MY FIRST BRITANNICA

People in History

4

ENCYCLOPÆDIA

Britannica®

CHICAGO   LONDON   NEW DELHI   PARIS   SEOUL   SYDNEY   TAIPEI   TOKYO

International Standard Book Number: 1-59339-048-3 (set)
International Standard Book Number: 1-59339-052-1 (volume 4)

My First Britannica:
Volume 4: People in History 2004

Britannica.com may be accessed on the Internet at http://www.britannica.com.

People in History

TABLE OF CONTENTS

Egyptian relief of Cleopatra VII
© Bettmann/Corbis

People in History

INTRODUCTION

Who is known as the Father of Europe?
What writer's name means 'two fathoms deep'?
How did Cleopatra die? Why did Gandhi march to the sea?

In Volume 4, *People in History,* you'll discover answers to these questions and many more. Through pictures, articles, and fun facts, you'll learn about the extraordinary people who have changed the course of history.

To help you on your journey, we've provided the following signposts in *People in History*:

■ **Subject Tabs**—The coloured box in the upper corner of each right-hand page will quickly tell you the article subject.

■ **Search Lights**—Try these mini-quizzes before and after you read the article and see how much - *and how quickly* - you can learn. You can even make this a game with a reading partner. (Answers are upside down at the bottom of one of the pages.)

■ **Did You Know?**—Check out these fun facts about the article subject. With these surprising 'factoids', you can entertain your friends, impress your teachers, and amaze your parents.

■ **Picture Captions**—Read the captions that go with the photos. They provide useful information about the article subject.

■ **Vocabulary**—New or difficult words are in **bold type**. You'll find them explained in the Glossary at the back of this volume. And there's a complete listing of all Glossary terms in the set in the ***Reference Guide and Index***, Volume 13.

■ **Learn More!**—Follow these pointers to related articles throughout the set.

And don't forget: If you're not sure where to start, where you saw something before, or where to go next, the ***Reference Guide and Index*** (Volume 13) will point the way.

Have a great trip!

MY FIRST BRITANNICA

© Ed Kashi/Corbis

The Letter Writer's Stories

Latin American writer Isabel Allende was born in 1942, in Lima, Peru. Her many books, written in Spanish, have been translated into several languages. Her works feature a **technique** called 'magic realism' - the use of fantasy and myth in realistic fiction. Her stories reflect her own experiences and also look at the role of women in Latin America.

Isabel Allende's uncle was Salvador Allende, president of Chile. She was a journalist there, as well as a short-story writer. In 1973, Salvador Allende was murdered during a time of political problems. Under the new government, Isabel Allende was threatened, and she and her husband and children were forced to flee to Venezuela. They ended up spending 13 years there.

Why do you suppose that Isabel Allende often writes about people who are exiles?

In 1981, while still in **exile**, she started writing a letter to her dying grandfather. She wrote about childhood memories and the people who had touched their lives. This letter turned into her first novel, *La casa de los espíritus* (1982; *The House of the Spirits*). It was followed by the novels *De amor y de sombra* (1984; *Of Love and Shadows*), *Eva Luna* (1987), and *El plan infinito* (1991; *The Infinite Plan*).

Most of Allende's stories have a political **aspect** and include a number of exiles. Allende calls these people the '**marginals**'. She says that they are exiled from the big umbrella of society. They have the courage to stand on the edge of life and not be sheltered or protected.

In 1990, Allende was able to return to Chile. But she was heartbroken when her young daughter became sick and died of a terrible blood disease. Out of her sorrow came a book, *Paula* (1994). It was Allende's first **non-fiction** book and it went on to become a bestseller.

LEARN MORE! READ THESE ARTICLES...
JORGE LUIS BORGES (VOLUME 3) • CHILE (VOLUME 9)
MYTHS AND LEGENDS, FOLKTALES AND FABLES (VOLUME 5)

Answer: Isabel Allende and her family became exiles themselves. It's not unusual for writers to draw on their own experiences for their work - even if it's fiction.

DID YOU KNOW?
Before he was a count, Basie was a baron. His first band was called the Barons of Rhythm.

An Aristocrat of Jazz

Young William Basie began studying music with his mother. He was later taught the organ by pianist Fats Waller. Waller himself was a well-known jazz musician.

Basie started his career playing piano on the vaudeville stage. Vaudeville was performed in a chain of theatres in the United States during the late 19th and early 20th centuries.

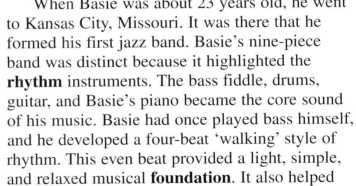

Count Basie in 1982.
© Roger Ressmeyer/Corbis

Vaudeville shows provided an entertaining mixture of dancing, singing, comedy, and magic acts.

When Basie was about 23 years old, he went to Kansas City, Missouri. It was there that he formed his first jazz band. Basie's nine-piece band was distinct because it highlighted the **rhythm** instruments. The bass fiddle, drums, guitar, and Basie's piano became the core sound of his music. Basie had once played bass himself, and he developed a four-beat 'walking' style of rhythm. This even beat provided a light, simple, and relaxed musical **foundation**. It also helped the harmonies and melodies in his songs stand out. Basie's rhythm section set the pattern that modern jazz accompanying styles would follow.

Basie and his band played at many nightclubs and often did radio broadcasts. One night a radio announcer called him 'Count' Basie, to liken him to another fine bandleader with an **aristocratic** nickname, Duke Ellington. From that point on the band gained in popularity.

The Basie band's popular early numbers included 'Lady Be Good', 'Shoe Shine Boy', 'One O'Clock Jump', and 'Jumpin' at the Woodside'. He formed another orchestra in the 1950s that was more **sophisticated**. Those musicians could read music and perform very difficult pieces. This group's hits included 'Alright, Okay, You Win' and 'April in Paris'.

LEARN MORE! READ THESE ARTICLES…
LOUIS ARMSTRONG (VOLUME 3) • JAZZ (VOLUME 3) • RADIO (VOLUME 2)

SEARCH LIGHT

True or false? Count Basie was a real count.

Answer: FALSE. 'Count' was Basie's nickname.

Writer of Life-Changing Stories

The famous English author Charles Dickens lived more than 100 years ago. Many of the stories he wrote were about how hard life could be for children. And many changes were made because of his books.

Some of Dickens' stories tell about how some children were treated badly in schools, at home, and at work. At his own school, his teacher beat

Charles Dickens.
© Bettmann/Corbis

him with a cane for laughing too loudly. Dickens was barely a teenager when he had to quit school and take a job away from home. His father had spent too much money and could not pay it back. He used many of his own experiences when he wrote his book *David Copperfield*.

When Dickens' stories were first read, some people were angry. Others were ashamed. Such stories as *Oliver Twist* made them think seriously. They realized that children should be treated kindly and should have fun as well as study hard. They should not be made to leave home and go to work when they are very young.

One of Dickens' best-known stories is called *A Christmas Carol*. It tells about a rich man called Scrooge who doesn't like Christmas. In fact, he doesn't like very much at all, except for making money. In the story, Scrooge learns that his life is better when he helps others and spends time enjoying their company.

People still like to read Dickens' books, not just to find out what life was like a long time ago but for the wonderful stories that they tell. Some are funny, like his *Pickwick Papers*. Some are family stories, such as *David Copperfield* and *Great Expectations*. And some of his books are historical stories, like *A Tale of Two Cities*.

LEARN MORE! READ THESE ARTICLES...
LEWIS CARROLL (VOLUME 3) • LITERATURE (VOLUME 3) • LONDON (VOLUME 6)

SEARCH LIGHT

True or false? Dickens' stories were entirely imaginary creations.

In this illustration from Dickens' *A Christmas Carol*, the miserly Ebenezer Scrooge is visited by the miserable ghost of his former partner, Jacob Marley.

© Bettmann/Corbis

Answer: FALSE. Dickens used experiences from his own life and the lives of unfortunate children for some of his stories.

DID YOU KNOW?
Elssler and her sister danced at Marie Taglioni's debut, in Taglioni's father's ballet troupe.

Theatrical Ballerina

Fanny Elssler was a famous Austrian dancer who brought energy and drama to her performances. She was born in 1810, in Vienna, Austria, and studied ballet from a young age. As a child, Elssler appeared with her sister in several ballets at Vienna's Kärntnerthor Theatre.

When she was a young adult, Elssler became famous worldwide thanks to her energetic spirit onstage and her remarkable pointe work (dancing on the points of the toes). She made her Paris Opéra debut in 1834 in Jean Coralli's ballet *La Tempête,* a dance version of William Shakespeare's play *The Tempest.*

Before Elssler came along, most ballet was 'classical ballet', which featured light graceful dance, like that performed by Elssler's greatest rival dancer, Marie Taglioni. But Elssler introduced theatrical, or 'character', ballet, which borrowed from folk dance traditions and even mime. She performed a Polish folk dance called the 'cracovienne' in the ballet *La Gypsy.* And because some Gypsies were associated with Spain, she got the nickname 'the Spaniard from the north'.

Elssler spent the later part of her career touring the United States, England, Germany, Italy, and Russia. Because of her long world tours, Elssler had to break her agreement with the Paris Opéra, and so she could not return to dance in France. Her worldwide tour ended up lasting more than ten years.

Elssler retired from the ballet in 1851. Her last years were spent in her native Vienna. During her career she was unequalled as a 'character' dancer with amazing dramatic powers.

LEARN MORE! READ THESE ARTICLES...
AUSTRIA (VOLUME 6) • DANCE (VOLUME 3) • MARIA TALLCHIEF (VOLUME 3)

Fanny Elssler was known for her great dramatic skill. She was one of the first ballerinas to tour the United States. She was noted for her Spanish dances and often performed with her sister Therese.
© Archivo Iconografico, S.A./Corbis

Painter to the King and to the People

As a young man in Spain, Francisco de Goya worked as a bull-fighter. But his great love was painting. After studying art in Rome, Goya returned to Spain and worked as a **tapestry** designer. Soon his talents attracted attention and he began painting portraits of wealthy Spaniards. By 1786 Goya had become a 'painter to the king of Spain'.

But Goya became tired of painting pictures of dukes and duchesses and the royal family. Most of the people of Spain were poor and often hungry.

Goya's self-portrait at the age of 69.
© Francis G. Mayer/Corbis

Constant wars made their lives worse. Wanting to portray this 'everyday' world, Goya began to draw and paint images of the poor and hardworking people of Spain.

Goya didn't make the men and women in his art look prettier or more important than they were. His paintings show people as they looked after a life of hard work. Goya included the lines in their faces and the sadness in their lives. He showed their bent backs and their worn clothes. This style of painting people and scenes from daily life is called 'realism'.

The subjects of Goya's paintings did not always please the king and the people of the royal court. They thought he should paint only famous people and beautiful things. In fact, his 'Disasters of War' series of etchings was so realistic and **gory** that it was not shown until over 35 years after Goya's death. But today, hundreds of years later, the power and honesty of Goya's 'everyday' paintings still impress and move viewers.

LEARN MORE! READ THESE ARTICLES…
MADRID (VOLUME 6) • PAINTING (VOLUME 3) • PABLO PICASSO (VOLUME 4)

SEARCH LIGHT

Why is Goya's art called 'realism'?

Goya's pictures of everyday life include some pleasant moments such as this one, titled 'Two Boys with Two Mastiffs'. (As you've probably guessed, a mastiff is a large breed of dog.)

Answer: Goya's painting style was called 'realism' because he showed ordinary people as they really were.

DID YOU KNOW?
In the late 1990s, some parents played Mozart for their babies, even while they were still in the womb. They thought Mozart's music would make children more intelligent, but there's no evidence to prove this notion.

A Life Filled with Music

When he was only 3 years old in Salzburg, Austria, Wolfgang Amadeus Mozart used to join his elder sister, Maria Anna, for her music lessons. But by the time he was 5, Mozart was making up his own music.

In the 18th century, when Mozart lived, most people didn't believe that a little boy could write such beautiful music. They thought Mozart's father had secretly written it.

So to test him, they asked young Mozart to stay in a room alone for a week. At the end of the week, Mozart had written a new piece of choir music. People agreed that this child was a musical genius.

Mozart studied, taught, played, and wrote music all his life. His music was often joyous, sometimes grim. But it was always beautiful. Mozart used the orchestra's players and instruments in ways no one else had done before.

SEARCH LIGHT

How old was Mozart when he began writing his own music?
a) 15
b) 5
c) 8

Music from Mozart's opera *Don Giovanni*.
© Bettmann/Corbis

Mozart often blended popular and classical music to create new styles of music, especially in the opera. He could compose in many musical styles and could play equally well on the organ, the harpsichord, the piano, and the violin. Mozart could hear a piece once and then play it from memory, sometimes rewriting and improving it as he played.

Although he died when he was still a young man, Mozart wrote 16 operas, 41 symphonies, and more than 500 other pieces of music. Some of his most famous works include the operas *The Marriage of Figaro*, *Don Giovanni*, and *The Magic Flute* and the 'Jupiter' Symphony.

LEARN MORE! READ THESE ARTICLES...
LUDWIG VAN BEETHOVEN (VOLUME 3) • CLASSICAL MUSIC (VOLUME 3)
JOAN SUTHERLAND (VOLUME 4)

Answer: b) 5

Grand Architect

Ieoh Ming Pei is one of the most important modern **architects**. He has created many major buildings throughout the world. And his style and ideas have strongly influenced the work of many other architects. He has specialized in building multi-storey structures in cities.

I.M. Pei on site during construction at the Louvre, Paris.
© Owen Franken/Corbis

I.M. Pei was born in Canton, China, in 1917. He went to America to study but couldn't return to China when World War II started. So most of his work has been in North America and Europe.

In the 1940s Pei began working as a professional architect. He worked on such important projects as the Mile High Center in Denver, Colorado.

In 1955 Pei formed his own architectural practice, I.M. Pei & Associates. The practice's early work included a museum in Syracuse, New York, that was actually four buildings joined by bridges. He also created a design for a new type of airport control tower that was widely used.

Pei's buildings are often tall, with lots of glass and steel. The designs combine simple **geometric** shapes, especially rectangles and triangles.

But his buildings are not dull or simple. In many of them, you can see the building supports or building materials, and these are their only decoration. The way that concrete, glass, and steel look together creates interesting designs on the sides of Pei's buildings. Special reflective glass also adds to the designs. He often combines different shapes and emphasizes the picture these shapes make in the **skyline**.

Some of Pei's most famous work includes the John Hancock Tower in Boston, the East Building of the National Gallery of Art in Washington, D.C., and the glass **pyramid** at the Louvre Museum in Paris, shown in the photograph here.

LEARN MORE! READ THESE ARTICLES…
ARCHITECTURE (VOLUME 3) • HASSAN FATHY (VOLUME 3)
MAYAN CIVILIZATION (VOLUME 4)

© Richard List/Corbis

DID YOU KNOW?

We think of the pyramids as being old stone structures in Egypt or Mexico. But Pei built a new glass pyramid as the entrance to the famous Louvre Museum in Paris just a few years ago.

Exploring with an Artist

SEARCH LIGHT

What does it mean to say that Picasso's studio was a jungle? (Hint: Jungles are hard to walk through.)

There's a story which says that the artist Pablo Picasso started to draw before he learned to speak. While this is probably only a story, it does suggest how important art was to Picasso.

Picasso was born in Spain in 1881 but lived much of his life in France. He was an inventor and an explorer. But he didn't invent machines or explore strange places. He explored and invented with art. He painted with his fingers, made drawings with a rusty nail, and even made a bull's head from the handlebars and seat of a bicycle. He was able to work anywhere at any time of the day or night.

Visitors viewing Picasso's painting 'Mandolin, Fruit Bowl, and Plaster Arm'.
© AFP/Corbis

Picasso's big studio was a sort of jungle - a jungle of paint cans, brushes, chalk, pottery, coloured pencils, and crayons, among many other things. Rolls of heavy paper and canvas, picture frames and easels, and tools for cutting designs on heavy board lay scattered about like rubbish. But to Picasso it was all **inspiration**.

He painted Spanish bullfighting, horse races, and clowns. He painted happy pictures in warm colours (such as pink) and sad, lonely ones in cool colours (such as dark blue). He sometimes painted people and animals the way they were. But more often he painted them from his imagination.

The art style that Picasso and fellow artist Georges Braque invented is called Cubism. They painted people and things so that all parts and sides could be seen at the same time. Cubists often created pictures from simple shapes such as squares or cubes.

LEARN MORE! READ THESE ARTICLES…
FRANCISCO DE GOYA (VOLUME 4) • PAINTING (VOLUME 3) • SPAIN (VOLUME 6)

In 2001 the works of Picasso were shown for the first time in China. These children are practising drawing by imitating some Picasso prints. A large photo of the artist looks on from the wall.
© Reuters NewMedia Inc./Corbis

DID YOU KNOW?
Picasso was probably the single most influential figure in 20th-century Western art. And he worked for 80 of his 91 years. He experimented with a large variety of styles in a number of artistic mediums.

Answer: Picasso's studio was so cluttered with art supplies that it was difficult to move around in it, Just as jungles are rich and dense with plant and animal life, so his studio was crowded with materials that helped him create.

Ætat. suæ. 34.

DID YOU KNOW?
Shakespeare was so imaginative in his use of language that he created, or 'coined', over 2,000 words or sayings that people have used ever since.

Plays That Never Grow Old

William Shakespeare is considered to be the greatest playwright in the English language and one of the most beloved playwrights in the world.

Not much is known about Shakespeare's life. He was born in Stratford-upon-Avon, England, in 1564. This was during the **reign** of Queen Elizabeth I. In his late 20s, Shakespeare went to the city of London to write and act. He joined a theatre **troupe** and began to write plays.

Over the next 20 years, Shakespeare wrote 38 plays and many poems. From his writing we can tell that he knew a lot about human feelings, as well as both city and country life. Most of the stories that Shakespeare told were known to his audience. But his characters and the way he told their stories in his plays attracted crowds of people to the Globe Theatre, where his troupe often performed.

2001 production of *A Midsummer Night's Dream* performed at the Albery Theatre in London.
© Archivo Iconografico, S.A./Corbis

Four hundred years later, people still enjoy reading Shakespeare's plays and seeing them onstage and in films. They quote his most famous lines (such as 'To be or not to be') and laugh and cry along with his characters. Shakespeare's plays have remained popular for several reasons. His characters show realistic human emotions. His **plots** are often complicated, but they always hold the audience's attention. And his language is powerful and poetic.

Some of Shakespeare's plays, such as *Hamlet*, have very sad endings. They are called 'tragedies'. Others, such as *A Midsummer Night's Dream*, are full of silly plots and have happy endings. They are the 'comedies'. Other Shakespeare plays, such as *Julius Caesar* or *Henry V*, are based on real-life figures and events. These are the 'histories'. And some plays, such as *Romeo and Juliet*, have a little bit of everything: romance, comedy, *and* tragedy.

LEARN MORE! READ THESE ARTICLES...
ELIZABETH I (VOLUME 4) • ENGLAND (VOLUME 6) • THEATRE (VOLUME 3)

William Shakespeare's plays have been popular for hundreds of years. Shown here is a portrait of the famous playwright.
© Robbie Jack/Corbis

SEARCH LIGHT

Which of the following describes a play with a happy ending?
a) tragedy
b) comedy
c) plot

23

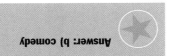
Answer: b) comedy

Teaching People to Think

Socrates was a thinker and teacher who lived in Athens, Greece, almost 2,500 years ago. Socrates knew all the famous people and leaders in Athens, but he didn't want to be famous or rich himself. He just wanted to think and to talk about ideas.

Socrates didn't give lectures or tell people what to think. Instead he asked questions. He thought it was very important to 'know yourself', and to learn how to be a good person and how to live a good life. Socrates talked to many people who thought they knew what was good and what was right. By asking them questions, Socrates made people think about things they hadn't noticed before.

Some people said that Socrates thought too much. Sometimes Socrates would stand in one place and think for many hours without moving or saying a word. Socrates didn't write down his thoughts and wasn't paid for his teaching. Socrates often angered people because he made them feel embarrassed when they could not answer his questions.

Eventually the leaders of Athens put Socrates in prison because they thought that he made young people misbehave and that he did not believe in the gods of Athens. As a punishment, they made Socrates drink a deadly poison. Socrates could have run away, but he chose to stay and accept his punishment. He believed he had a duty to obey the law. One of Socrates' students, Plato, became a famous teacher himself. He wrote down many of Socrates' conversations so that his ideas would be preserved for many future generations.

LEARN MORE! READ THESE ARTICLES...
ATHENS (VOLUME 6) • CONFUCIUS (VOLUME 5) • ALBERT EINSTEIN (VOLUME 4)

DID YOU KNOW?
Socrates' method of asking questions to teach new ideas is still used in schools today. It is called the 'Socratic method'.

Socrates is often admired for holding on to his views even though it cost him his life. Sometimes, as here, the great thinker is celebrated in art.
© Araldo de Luca/Corbis

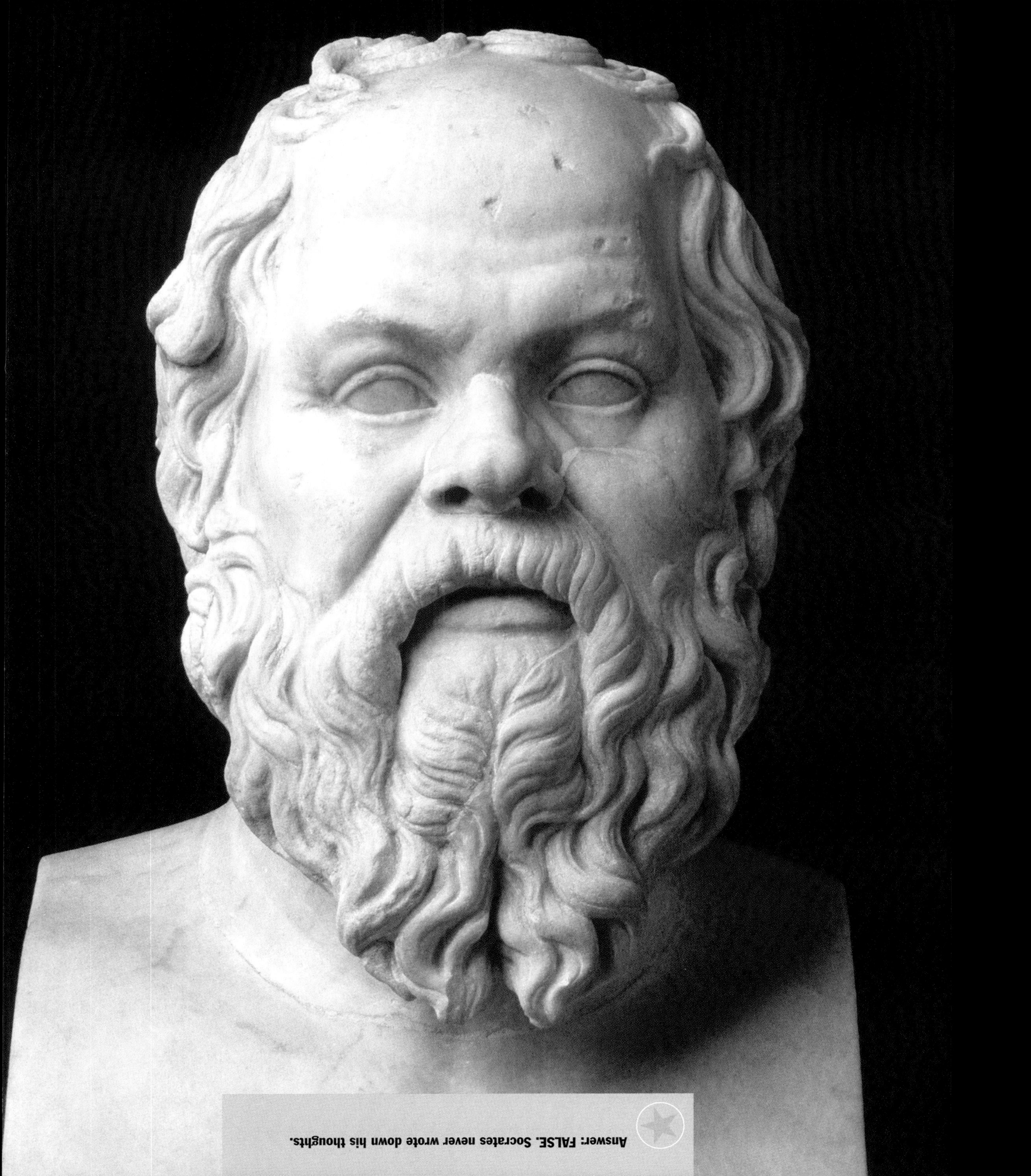

Answer: FALSE. Socrates never wrote down his thoughts.

SEARCH LIGHT

True
or false?
Joan Sutherland
never needed any
training to become a
great singer.

Australia's Golden Voice

Opera singer Joan Sutherland was born in Sydney, Australia, on 7 November 1926. She was a musical child and studied piano and music with her mother. At about age 20 Sutherland won a singing competition and began studying professionally.

A year later Sutherland made her first appearance as a singer in a performance of Henry Purcell's opera *Dido and Aeneas*. She played the lead female role of Dido.

Sutherland won many prizes in singing competitions, and she used the money to move to London. There she studied at the Royal College of Music. In 1952 she became a member of the company of the Royal Opera, Covent Garden. She made her first appearance there in Wolfgang Amadeus Mozart's *The Magic Flute*.

In 1961 Sutherland performed in Gaetano Donizetti's *Lucia di Lammermoor* at the **Metropolitan** Opera, New York City. Lucia was a difficult role. On one hand it required the singer to do some extremely tricky vocal **gymnastics**. In addition to that, it was a major acting challenge. Sutherland performed it so well that her fame spread around the world. She was soon performing in major opera houses all over Europe.

Sutherland was admired as a coloratura soprano. Sopranos are female singers with very high voices. Coloratura singers have to have a very light and flexible voice. They must be able to sing complex series of notes very rapidly.

Sutherland was one of the most successful opera stars of her day. In 1978 she was knighted as a Dame Commander of the British Empire. She retired from the stage in 1990, at the age of 64.

LEARN MORE! READ THESE ARTICLES...
AUSTRALIA (VOLUME 7) • OPERA (VOLUME 3)
KIRI TE KANAWA (VOLUME 3)

DID YOU KNOW?
Sutherland's nickname to her fans was 'La Stupenda' because of her stupendous (fantastic) talent.

Answer: FALSE. Sutherland continued to train throughout her career.

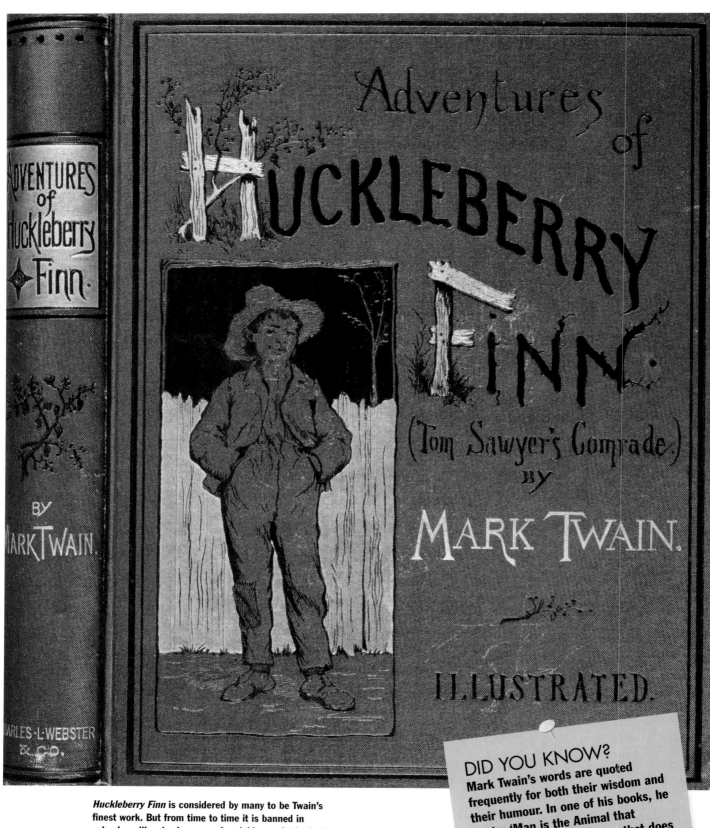

Huckleberry Finn is considered by many to be Twain's finest work. But from time to time it is banned in schools or libraries because of racial issues in the book.

DID YOU KNOW?
Mark Twain's words are quoted frequently for both their wisdom and their humour. In one of his books, he wrote: 'Man is the Animal that Blushes. He is the only one that does it - or has occasion to.' What do you suppose he meant?

The Writer and the Mississippi River

A one time Mississippi River boat pilot, Mark Twain became one of America's greatest authors. His *Tom Sawyer*, *Huckleberry Finn*, and *Life on the Mississippi* rank high on any list of great American books.

Mark Twain was born Samuel Langhorne Clemens in 1835. He grew up in Hannibal, Missouri, on the Mississippi River. From this river town he gathered the material for his most famous stories. Young Tom Sawyer, for instance, was a combination of several boys - including himself.

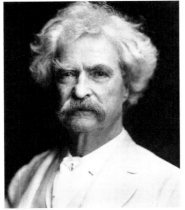

Mark Twain.
© Bettmann/Corbis

During his life, he held jobs that he would turn into material for his writing. His work as a riverboat pilot gave him experience he used to write *Life on the Mississippi*. When he began working as a newspaper reporter, he began using the pen-name Mark Twain. It is an old river term meaning two fathoms, or 12 feet, of water - a depth that was not very safe for riverboats.

One of his stories, 'The Celebrated Jumping Frog of Calaveras County', was printed in many newspapers. It was a popular story, and Twain travelled as a roving reporter and then on a lecture tour. After these travels he wrote *The Innocents Abroad*, which made him famous.

Twain was known as a humourist. But behind his mask of humour lay a serious view of life. He had known the sadness of poverty, the early death of his father and later his brother Henry, and the loss of a daughter. One of his most famous novels, *Huckleberry Finn*, is sometimes thought of as a child's book. But its heartbreak and wisdom are appreciated best by adults. Another of his famous novels, *Tom Sawyer*, is mostly a young person's book that adults can also read with pleasure.

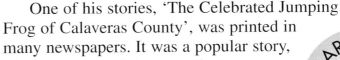

SEARCH LIGHT

'Half twain' means 'mark twain plus half a mark' and equals 15 feet. So how much is a mark?

LEARN MORE! READ THESE ARTICLES...
CHARLES DICKENS (VOLUME 4) • FROGS (VOLUME 11) • SHIPS (VOLUME 2)

Answer: A mark equals 6 feet. Mark twain, 12 feet, is two marks. Half twain is 2 1/2 marks, or 15 feet.

Leader of the Palestinians

Since he was a teenager in the 1940s, Yasir Arafat has been involved with the Palestinian movement. Israel was formed after World War II to give the Jewish people a homeland. But its creation moved hundreds of thousands of Palestinian Arabs off their land. After 1948 Palestinians such as Arafat wanted to get that land back by fighting against Israel. To do this they formed the Palestine **Liberation** Organization (PLO).

For years Arafat led a group that was part of the PLO. The group carried out deadly attacks on Israel. Israel responded by attacking the Palestinians. Arafat became **chairman** of the

Yasir Arafat in 1990.
© David Turnley/Corbis

PLO in 1969. He wanted the PLO to work for change through discussion and bargaining more than by force. Arafat worked to get countries around the world to accept the idea of a Palestinian homeland.

In 1993 the PLO agreed to accept Israel's right to exist as a country as long as the Palestinians were allowed to rule themselves. With help from other countries, Arafat and Israeli Prime Minister Yitzhak Rabin signed agreements to make peace between the two sides. The next year Arafat, Rabin, and Israeli Foreign Minister Shimon Peres shared the Nobel Prize for Peace for their work together.

However, the peace agreements between the two sides weakened. Rabin was assassinated by an Israeli, and Arafat could not work easily with other Israeli leaders. Serious violence finally broke out in 2000. Arafat could not or would not stop terrorist attacks by Palestinian radicals. Some world leaders have tried to get Arafat to step down as leader of the Palestinians because of the violence.

LEARN MORE! READ THESE ARTICLES…
MENACHEM BEGIN (VOLUME 4) • ISRAEL (VOLUME 7)
MOHAMMED ALI JINNAH (VOLUME 4)

DID YOU KNOW?
Arafat's full name is Muhammad 'Abd al-Ra'uf al-Qudwah al-Husayni. Yasir is a nickname that means 'easy'.

These Palestinian policemen carry a poster of Yasir Arafat. To many Palestinians, Arafat has long symbolized their hope for a return to the land that became Israel after World War II.
© AFP/Corbis

The Emperor
and the Right Way of Living

Some 2,200 years ago the emperor Ashoka ruled India. Like many ancient rulers, he expanded his empire by conquering new lands. But unlike most rulers, Ashoka suddenly turned his back on warfare and began to govern according to the non-violent beliefs of Buddhism.

It is said that Ashoka became a Buddhist when he saw the horrors caused by the wars he'd led. After that, he decided to serve his subjects and all humanity instead of conquering others. He called this 'conquest by *dharma*'. In India *dharma* means the 'right way of living' and 'universal truth'. This includes being honest, truthful, and kind. It also means being merciful, generous, and thoughtful.

The emperor himself would often tour the countryside, preaching his belief in *dharma* to the people. Ashoka also appointed '*dharma* ministers' to help relieve people's sufferings. These ministers were assigned to look after the special needs of women and people living in religious communities.

Ashoka passed laws to prevent cruelty to animals and had hospitals built for both people and animals. He also started construction projects to make all people's lives easier. Trees were planted on roadsides, wells were dug, and watering sheds and rest houses were built.

The only recognition Ashoka wanted was for people to remember that he had ruled according to *dharma*. To preserve his ideas, Ashoka had his teachings carved on rocks and pillars (columns) in public areas. These inscriptions are called the Rock **Edicts** and Pillar Edicts. The most famous is the lion pillar found at Sarnath, which has become India's national emblem.

SEARCH LIGHT

Ashoka was an Indian
a) mathematician.
b) emperor.
c) priest.

DID YOU KNOW?
Despite his reputation as a kind and generous ruler, some stories describe Ashoka as cruel and ruthless. According to one story, he had all his brothers killed in order to seize the throne.

LEARN MORE! READ THESE ARTICLES...
BUDDHISM (VOLUME 5)
CHARLEMAGNE (VOLUME 4) • INDIA (VOLUME 7)

Sarnath, an archaeological site in northern India, is said to be the place where the Buddha first preached to his followers. Ashoka built this *stupa* (shrine) and others, as well as pillars, to honour the event.
© Brian A. Vikander/Corbis

ASHOKA

Menachem Begin visited the Western Wall in Jerusalem to offer a prayer of thanks following his 1981 election victory.

Struggling for Israel

Menachem Begin in 1981.
© Bettmann/Corbis

When Menachem Begin was a little boy growing up in Poland, he probably never imagined that someday he would lead a Jewish nation and win a Nobel Prize for Peace.

As a young man, Menachem earned a law degree and became an active Zionist. Members of the Zionist movement wanted to create a Jewish community in the Middle Eastern region of Palestine.

Germany invaded Poland early in World War II, and the Nazis began to **persecute** the Jews. Begin joined the Polish army in **exile**. He went with them to Palestine in 1942. There Begin joined a group fighting to create a Jewish state. However, after the creation of the State of Israel in 1948, hundreds of thousands of Palestinian Arabs either left or were forced off their land. This led to many years of trouble between Israel and the Arab countries that surround it.

Begin was active in Israeli politics in the 1950s and '60s, and in 1977 he became the country's **prime minister**. By that time Israel had fought several wars with the Arabs and had captured some Arab land. Begin signed a peace treaty with Egyptian leader Anwar el-Sadat, returning Egypt's land. This earned Begin and Sadat the Nobel Prize for Peace in 1978. But Begin refused to accept the demands by Palestinians for a return of lands that he considered part of Israel.

Four years later he ordered Israeli troops to invade Lebanon and attack Palestinian guerrillas. The war in Lebanon was very unpopular in Israel, and Begin stepped down as prime minister in 1983.

LEARN MORE! READ THESE ARTICLES...
ISRAEL (VOLUME 7) • GOLDA MEIR (VOLUME 4)
ANWAR EL-SADAT (VOLUME 4)

DID YOU KNOW?

Menachem Begin and Anwar el-Sadat's 1978 peace agreement is known as the Camp David Accords. Camp David is the getaway spot where U.S. President Jimmy Carter took the two men to help them work toward peace.

DID YOU KNOW?
In William Shakespeare's play *Julius Caesar*, Caesar is told to 'beware the ides of March'. The ides refers to the time around the 15th of the month. Today those famous words are sometimes used as a warning.

Rome's Remarkable General and Statesman

Julius Caesar was a brilliant general and a gifted writer. But most important, he helped create the ancient Roman Empire.

Early in his career Caesar formed a **bond** with the two most powerful men in Rome - the wealthy Crassus and the general Pompey. In 59 BC

Sculpture of Julius Caesar, in the National Museum in Naples.
© Bettmann/Corbis

they helped elect Caesar as one of Rome's two consuls, the government's highest rank. After a year as consul, Caesar left Rome to govern Gaul (now France). There he earned a reputation as a military leader. He stopped uprisings and invasions, and he even landed in Britain. Caesar also wrote detailed accounts of his battles.

While Caesar was in Gaul, Crassus was killed. Pompey now controlled Rome and he turned against Caesar. He declared Caesar a criminal and ordered him to break up his army. Instead, Caesar declared war and marched to Rome. Pompey fled to Greece.

At that time Rome was governed by a senate (a supreme council). But Caesar felt the government was corrupt and needed a strong leader. In 49 BC he declared himself **dictator**, and he spent five years fighting a civil war against Pompey to make his rule secure. Some of the Roman senators worried that Caesar had too much power. On 15 March 44 BC they murdered Caesar on the floor of the Senate.

In the short time he led Rome, Caesar proved to be a great statesman. The changes he made helped begin the 500-year Roman Empire. And for almost 2,000 years after his death, some world leaders used a form of the title 'caesar' (such as 'Kaiser' in Germany and 'czar' in Russia).

LEARN MORE! READ THESE ARTICLES...
CHARLEMAGNE (VOLUME 4) • ITALY (VOLUME 6) • ROME (VOLUME 6)

By crossing over the stream known as the Rubicon in 49 BC, Caesar basically declared war against the Roman senate. 'Crossing the Rubicon', the subject of this engraving, became a phrase that means taking a step from which there's no turning back.
© Bettmann/Corbis

SEARCH LIGHT

Fill in the gap: Caesar took power in Rome after defeating

_____,

his former political supporter.

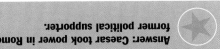

Answer: Caesar took power in Rome after defeating Pompey, his former political supporter.

37

DID YOU KNOW?
Castro was a very good baseball player. It is said he once even tried out for the Senators, a professional baseball team in Washington, D.C.

The Man Who Changed Cuba

In the 1950s General Fulgencio Batista ruled the Caribbean island of Cuba. His rule was harsh and often violent, and some large American companies grew rich while many Cubans remained poor. Fidel Castro was a young lawyer who believed Batista's rule was unfair. There were no free elections in Cuba, so Castro organized a military force to overthrow Batista.

Castro bought guns with his own money and attacked Batista's forces in 1953. The attack failed badly, and after two years in prison Castro went to Mexico to make a new plan. Soon he and about 80 other **rebels** arrived in Cuba. They hid in the mountains and fought a **guerrilla** war using small-scale battles and making hit-and-run attacks. Batista finally fled Cuba in 1959.

Castro became Cuba's leader and created a **communist** government to

Fidel Castro in 1960.
© Bettmann/Corbis

control all parts of Cuba's life. After a while, the people lost many of the same rights that Batista had taken away, and Cuban businesses did not create new wealth. Many Cubans left their homeland or tried to do so. But Castro also greatly increased many benefits to the Cuban people. Education and health services were free, and every citizen was guaranteed work.

The United States, Cuba's near neighbour, strongly opposed Castro's government. They even tried to overthrow it in 1961. And in 1962 Cuba was at the centre of a dangerous clash between the United States and the **Soviet Union**. Castro had let Soviet **nuclear weapons** be set up in Cuba.

Today Cuba is one of the last communist countries in the world. In the late 20th century there was unrest among Cubans, and Castro relaxed some of his strictest controls. Still, after more than 40 years, he remains Cuba's powerful leader.

LEARN MORE! READ THESE ARTICLES...
SIMÓN BOLÍVAR (VOLUME 4) • CUBA (VOLUME 9) • MAO ZEDONG (VOLUME 4)

SEARCH LIGHT

True or false? The United States has supported Castro's rule in Cuba.

Fidel Castro still speaks out strongly against people who disagree with his communist government in Cuba. Here he speaks at a rally in 2003.
© AFP/Corbis

Answer: FALSE. Since the early 1960s, the United States has opposed Castro and has supported attempts to overthrow him.

Dis ist der gstalt und biltnus gläch

kaiser karols der das römisch reich den teutschen under trug mach

kaxolus jmpaint

magnus Annis .14 2

Nürenberg alle Jar · mit andern haltrun offenbar

DID YOU KNOW?
Charlemagne enjoyed swimming. He even built a palace on a hot spring that he used for bathing with friends.

Charlemagne's empire survived for only a brief time after he died. But no other ruler in the European Middle Ages had such a deep and long-lasting effect.
© Ali Meyer/Corbis

The Father of Europe

During the Middle Ages (about AD 500-1500) one of the most powerful European kings was Charlemagne. Charlemagne was a Frank. The Franks were a people who lived in parts of modern France and Germany. When he became the one and only ruler of the Frankish lands in AD 771, Charlemagne wanted to make his kingdom bigger and stronger. He also wanted to spread Christianity and protect the Roman Catholic church.

With this plan in mind, Charlemagne spent 30 years battling the Saxons, another Germanic people. In these and many other wars, Charlemagne gained control over much of western Europe, including what is now France, Switzerland, Belgium, the Netherlands, and half of Italy and Germany.

In the year 800, the **pope** crowned Charlemagne the emperor of the Romans. This made him the first of many emperors who would rule until

Illuminated (richly decorated) manuscript showing Charlemagne meeting Pope Adrian I.
© Archivo Iconografico, S.A./Corbis

1806. Charlemagne reorganized the government in his empire. He worked with leaders of the church to improve the church and government. And he sent out special agents to ensure that his laws were being obeyed.

Charlemagne brought about many improvements in the kingdom. He set up a new money system and reformed the law courts. He built a large court library and set up a school at his palace court. He was concerned with educating the ordinary people and improving the learning of priests. He hoped education would make his people better Christians.

Charlemagne died in 814. Today he is remembered as one of the most important rulers in European history. In fact, he's sometimes called the father of Europe.

LEARN MORE! READ THESE ARTICLES...
ASHOKA (VOLUME 3) • EUROPE (VOLUME 6) • MUHAMMAD (VOLUME 5)

SEARCH LIGHT

Which of these did Charlemagne **not** build?
a) pyramids
b) schools
c) libraries

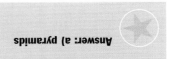

Answer: a) pyramids

Queen of Egypt

She spoke nine languages, was a good mathematician, and had a great head for business. And she would use both her intelligence and her beauty to hold on to power. Today, Cleopatra VII Thea Philopator of Egypt is still an amazing historical figure.

Cleopatra was the second daughter of King Ptolemy XII. When her father died in 51 BC, 18-year-old Cleopatra was supposed to rule Egypt with her 15-year-old brother, Ptolemy XIII. In a few years, her brother's supporters drove Cleopatra from power. But later the Roman leader Julius Caesar helped her get her throne back. War soon broke out. In 47 BC Cleopatra's brother and co-ruler drowned. By law she couldn't rule alone, so she married her 11-year-old brother.

Cleopatra returned to Rome to live with Caesar and had a son by him named Caesarion. But Caesar was murdered in 44 BC, and Cleopatra lost her strongest supporter. She soon went back to Egypt. With Caesar dead, the two most powerful men in Rome were Octavian and Mark Antony. When Antony wanted to invade Persia, he invited Cleopatra to meet him.

Antony quickly fell in love with Cleopatra and married her. But he was also married to Octavian's sister. An angry Octavian declared war against Antony and eventually defeated him. Antony died in Cleopatra's arms.

Cleopatra did not want to live without Antony. The story is that she had an asp (a kind of snake) brought to her, and when it bit her, Cleopatra died at the age of 39. The Egyptians believed that death by snakebite made you **immortal**. Cleopatra didn't live forever, but her legend has lasted more than 2,000 years.

LEARN MORE! READ THESE ARTICLES...
JULIUS CAESAR (VOLUME 4) • EGYPT (VOLUME 8)
WILLIAM SHAKESPEARE (VOLUME 4)

SEARCH LIGHT

How many times did Cleopatra rule Egypt?

DID YOU KNOW?
William Shakespeare wrote a play about Egypt's most famous queen, called *Antony and Cleopatra.*

This image of the Egyptian queen Cleopatra appears on a temple of the goddess Hathor in Dandarah, Egypt. Hathor was the goddess of the sky, of women, and of love.
The Art Archive

A Clever, Courageous Queen

When Elizabeth I became queen of England, few thought she would last very long. But Elizabeth I not only ruled for almost half a century. She became one of England's greatest rulers.

Elizabeth was the daughter of Anne Boleyn, King Henry VIII's second wife. Henry also had a daughter, Mary, from his first marriage, and had a son, Edward, from his third. After Henry's death, Edward ruled for a short time until he died. Mary ruled for three years before she too died. In 1558 Elizabeth became the queen of England at the age 25.

Oil painting of Elizabeth I with members of her court.
© Stapleton Collection/Corbis

At the time, England was poor, weak, and torn by **conflict** between different groups. The people hoped Elizabeth would marry a strong man who would guide her. But Elizabeth had no desire to share her power. She was determined to be a successful queen, so she gathered experienced and trustworthy advisers. Elizabeth herself had a good education and was very clever and courageous.

The queen encouraged English sailors to travel to distant parts of the world. Captains such as Francis Drake brought back riches and found new trade routes to the Americas, Asia, and Africa. As trade developed with other lands, England grew wealthy. Under Elizabeth, England also experienced a Renaissance, or 'rebirth' of the arts. Some of the famous writers of the period were William Shakespeare, Christopher Marlowe, Francis Bacon, Edmund Spenser, and John Donne.

By the time Elizabeth died in 1603, England had become both rich and strong. The 45 years of her **reign** became known as the Elizabethan Age.

LEARN MORE! READ THESE ARTICLES...
CLEOPATRA (VOLUME 4) • JUDI DENCH (VOLUME 3) • ENGLAND (VOLUME 6)

Elizabeth I, popularly known as Good Queen Bess, became queen after the death of her half sister in 1558. She loved showy clothing and jewels.
© Archivo Iconografico, S.A./Corbis

DID YOU KNOW?
During Elizabeth's rule, Spain attacked England with a great fleet of ships called the Spanish Armada. England's victory over the Spanish forces saved the country from becoming part of the Spanish empire.

SEARCH LIGHT

Elizabeth ruled England only after her
a) two sisters ruled.
b) sister and brother ruled.
c) two brothers ruled.

Answer: b) sister and brother ruled.

大清當今慈禧端佑康頤昭豫莊誠壽恭欽獻崇熙聖母皇太后

The Dragon Lady

One of the most powerful women in Chinese history was Cixi. She controlled China for more than 40 years in the late 1800s. Cixi was so **ruthless** and dangerous that some people called her the Dragon Lady.

In Western countries such as Great Britain and the United States, Cixi was also known as the Empress Dowager. But she was never really an empress. She was just the mother of the emperor's only son. When the emperor died, she helped her 6-year-old son, who was heir to the throne, rule China. She still had power when her son was old enough to rule by himself. Then he died, and the Dragon Lady made sure her 4-year-old nephew became the new emperor. This was against the law, but she helped him rule too.

The Dragon Lady lived in a group of palace buildings called the Forbidden City, within the city of Beijing. Only the servants who lived there too ever saw Cixi. She spoke to all her visitors from a large red throne shaped like a dragon that was hidden behind a silk screen. Every one of her orders ended with the warning 'Hear and obey'.

Under Cixi the Chinese government became very dishonest. Many believed that Cixi had had many people murdered. In 1908, when the Dragon Lady was dying, she had her nephew, the emperor, poisoned. She wanted to make sure that he died first and thus would never rule without her.

SEARCH LIGHT

Did anybody ever see the Empress of China?

DID YOU KNOW?

The Dragon Lady wore solid gold shields on her very long fingernails to keep them from breaking.

LEARN MORE! READ THESE ARTICLES...
CHINA (VOLUME 7) • CLEOPATRA (VOLUME 4)
MAO ZEDONG (VOLUME 4)

Known in the West as the Empress Dowager, Cixi controlled the political life of China for many decades. The nation was fairly stable under her influence, but the government was dishonest and did not make changes that were needed to benefit the people.
© Hulton-Deutsch Collection/Corbis

Answer: Only the servants living within the Forbidden City ever saw the Empress of China.

47

Hirohito ruled over the island nation of
a) Britain.
b) Indonesia.
c) Japan.

48

Emperor of Japan

Michinomiya Hirohito was the last of the old-style **emperors** of Japan. He helped usher in a new age for the Japanese people. He was born in 1901, and he was the first Japanese **crown prince** to travel abroad.

Emperor Hirohito in 1982.
© Bettmann/Corbis

Hirohito became emperor of Japan on 25 December 1926, after his father's death. At that time the military was gaining control of the government and would soon take Japan into a major war in Asia. Eventually Japan crossed the Pacific and attacked Hawaii and the Philippines, which brought the United States into World War II. Historians still don't agree about whether the emperor actually wanted a war with the United States or if he just couldn't stop the military chiefs.

By 1945 Japan was nearing defeat, and Hirohito favoured ending the war. On 15 August 1945, he broadcast his country's surrender on the radio. It was the first time the Japanese people had heard their emperor's voice.

After the war Hirohito made many changes. Until then, Japanese emperors had claimed to be descended from gods. Hirohito now gave up this claim. The old **constitution** had also given the emperor highest authority. A new constitution gave power to the people.

The emperor also started appearing before the Japanese public. He allowed the press to photograph and write about him and his family. In 1959 he permitted his son, Crown Prince Akihito, to marry a **commoner**, which was a major break with tradition. Hirohito helped Japan build relationships with countries all over the world.

Hirohito's health began to fail as he grew older. He died on 7 January 1989.

LEARN MORE! READ THESE ARTICLES...
EMPRESS OF CHINA (VOLUME 3)
JAPAN: MODERN NATION OF ANCIENT TRADITIONS (VOLUME 7)
SHINTO (VOLUME 5)

> ## DID YOU KNOW?
> According to tradition, 123 emperors ruled over Japan before Hirohito. Yet Hirohito ruled the longest - he was the emperor of Japan for 63 years.

After World War II, Emperor Hirohito tried to bring the imperial family closer to the Japanese people. He began to appear in public more often and allowed pictures and stories of his personal and family life to be published.
© Corbis

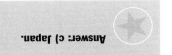

Answer: c) Japan.

Founder of Pakistan

Mohammed Ali Jinnah was born in Karachi in 1876. At that time the city was part of India, and India was controlled by the British. When Jinnah was a young man, his parents sent him to London to gain business experience. Instead, he studied law and learned about the British system of government. After his studies, he returned to India and began to practice law in Bombay (now Mumbai). It was about this time that the people of India began to seek freedom from British rule.

Mohammed Ali Jinnah.
© Bettmann/Corbis

For hundreds of years, Muslims and Hindus - the area's two major religious groups - had lived together peacefully in India. But there were many more Hindus than Muslims. Because of this, many Muslims feared that they might not be treated equally once India became an independent country.

Although Jinnah was Muslim, at first he didn't think there was anything to be afraid of. But as time passed, he began to feel that the Muslims in India should have their own country. So Jinnah began to work hard to make a Muslim nation out of part of India's land. The new country would be called Pakistan.

In 1947 the British government agreed to the formation of Pakistan. India became independent from Britain in August of that year, and a section of the country became Pakistan. Jinnah was chosen as Pakistan's first head of state, but he served for only a year before he died. Despite his short rule, Jinnah's people loved him. And because he helped create Pakistan, Jinnah is considered the Father of Pakistan.

LEARN MORE! READ THESE ARTICLES...
MAHATMA GANDHI (VOLUME 4) • ISLAM (VOLUME 5) • PAKISTAN (VOLUME 7)

SEARCH LIGHT

For which people did Jinnah want to build a country?

Mohammed Ali Jinnah founded the state of Pakistan in 1947. Here, Pakistani soldiers in 1993 hang a portrait of Jinnah as part of preparations for Pakistan Day in March.
© Reuters NewMedia Inc./Corbis

DID YOU KNOW?
In 1993 Nelson Mandela and F.W. de Klerk were jointly awarded the Nobel Prize for Peace for ending the apartheid system.

A Fighter for Rights

South African leader Nelson Mandela was a fighter. He fought against apartheid. Apartheid was an official policy of the government of South Africa that separated people according to their race and colour.

During World War II, Mandela joined the African National Congress (ANC), and he later became one of its leaders. This organization had one aim - to fight for the freedom of the black people in South Africa.

True or false? Mandela spent his life in prison.

Mandela didn't want to use violence in the ANC's fight against the government. However, after the police killed unarmed Africans, Mandela changed his mind. He argued for using **sabotage** against the government - that is, secretly working to undermine and destroy it. At the same time, the South African government outlawed the ANC. In 1962 the government decided that Mandela was guilty of acts against the government. He was sentenced to five years in prison. The following year, he was found guilty of more charges and sentenced to life imprisonment.

Nelson Mandela in 1990.
© David Turnley/Corbis

By the 1980s, more and more people had heard about Mandela's hopes for South Africa. They began to **campaign** for his release from prison. Countries and organizations all over the world gave him their support. Early in 1990, South Africa's president, F.W. de Klerk, ordered Mandela's release. President de Klerk, together with Mandela, worked to change South Africa into a country where all races would have equal rights.

South Africa held its first elections open to people of all races in 1994. Mandela and the ANC won the elections, and Mandela became the country's first black president.

LEARN MORE! READ THESE ARTICLES…
MAHATMA GANDHI (VOLUME 4) • MARTIN LUTHER KING, JR. (VOLUME 4)
SOUTH AFRICA: A PEOPLE APART (VOLUME 8)

Nelson Mandela spent nearly 30 years of his life as a political prisoner. Four years after his release he ran for president of South Africa. He was elected in April 1994.
© Peter Turnley/Corbis

Answer: FALSE. He served a large part of his life - almost 30 years.

Architect of Modern China

Mao Zedong was born in 1893 in China's Hunan province. Mao's father had been born a poor peasant, but he became wealthy as a farmer and grain dealer. Only limited education was available where Mao grew up. So, at the age of 13, he left school to work on his family's farm. He

Mao Zedong in 1967.
© Bettmann/Corbis

later ran away to attend school in the provincial capital, where he discovered new ideas from Chinese and Western thinkers.

Mao briefly served in the army during the Chinese Revolution (1911-12). This uprising overthrew the ruling Manchu **dynasty** and turned China into a **republic**. After that there were many years of fighting between different groups who wanted to rule China. This time was known as the 'warlord period'.

After the war, Mao returned to school, ending up at Beijing University, where he worked in the library. There he became involved in the May Fourth Movement of 1919. This was the beginning of China's move towards communism. In communism, property is owned by the state or community, and all citizens are supposed to have a share in the nation's wealth.

In the 1920s, Mao helped create the Chinese Communist Party (CCP). He started a communist revolution among peasants in the countryside. The CCP broke away from the Nationalist Party. The Nationalists thought that the Chinese should decide their own future, but they opposed communism. The Red Army, Mao's military force, began fighting them and gathering strength in the late 1920s.

Mao finally took control of the whole country in 1949 and became the chairman of the People's Republic of China. Although the lives of many poor people were improved under Mao, many others suffered and died during his efforts at reform and improvement. He died on September 9, 1976.

SEARCH LIGHT

Was Mao's family rich or poor?

LEARN MORE! READ THESE ARTICLES...
CHARLEMAGNE (VOLUME 4) • CHINA (VOLUME 7)
CONFUCIUS (VOLUME 5)

Mao Zedong, the leader of the Chinese communists, spent a great deal of time in the countryside trying to gain support for his ideas. Here, as a young man, he speaks to a group of his followers.
© Bettmann/Corbis

Answer: Actually, they were both. His father was born poor but later became a wealthy farmer and merchant.

Israel's First Woman Prime Minister

In 1906, when Goldie Mabovitch was a child, poverty forced her family to move from Russia to the United States to find work. At school, she

Israeli Prime Minister Golda Meir in 1972.
© Hulton-Deutsch Collection/Corbis

joined a group that wanted Jews to have their own country. This was known as Zionism. A few years later she and her husband, Morris Myerson, moved to Palestine, a Middle Eastern region then under British control.

Goldie Myerson became involved in political activities in Palestine. She **negotiated** protection for Jews who fled from Nazi Europe during World War II. After the war, she worked to help Jewish war refugees.

In 1948 part of Palestine became the State of Israel, and Goldie Myerson was one of the signers of Israel's declaration of independence. The surrounding Arab countries attacked Israel, but the new country defended itself and remained independent.

The following year she was elected to the Knesset, the Israeli **parliament**. Later she changed her last name from Myerson to 'Meir', a Hebrew word meaning 'to burn brightly'. She also became known as 'Golda' instead of Goldie.

Meir became the prime minister of Israel in February 1969. As prime minister, she worked hard for peace in the Middle East and travelled widely to meet with the leaders of many other countries.

But in 1973 Egypt and Syria's invasion of Israel led to another Arab-Israeli war. Though Israel eventually won the war, the whole country was stunned by the attack. Many Israelis felt Meir's government was to blame, and so she resigned as prime minister the following year.

LEARN MORE! READ THESE ARTICLES...
MENACHEM BEGIN (VOLUME 4) • ISRAEL (VOLUME 7)
JUDAISM (VOLUME 5)

DID YOU KNOW?
Golda Meir was 71 years old when she became the world's third female prime minister. The first two were Sirimavo R.D. Bandaranaike of Ceylon (now Sri Lanka) and Indira Gandhi of India.

Before she became Israel's prime minister, Golda Meir served as Israel's representative to the United Nations. In this photo, Meir helps a little girl light five candles to celebrate Israel's fifth anniversary.
© Bettmann/Corbis

Answer: Knesset, Palestine, Israel

SEARCH LIGHT

True or false? Sadat did not want Egypt to be run by a king.

Egypt's Man of Peace

When Muhammad Anwar el-Sadat was born in 1918, Egypt was still a British colony and was ruled by a sultan. But one day Sadat would rise to become Egypt's president.

Sadat was in the army during World War II. After that he joined an organization that wanted to overthrow the Egyptian **monarchy** and drive

Anwar el-Sadat, reviewing a military parade, shortly before he was killed.
© Kevin Fleming/Corbis

out the British. The organization was led by Gamal Abdel Nasser. In 1952 Nasser's group was successful, and Egypt gained its independence. Nasser became the country's first president, and Sadat twice served as his vice-president. When Nasser died in 1970, Sadat became president.

Egypt had lost control of the land lying between Egypt and Israel during a war with Israel in 1967. The two countries remained enemies after that. In six years Sadat ordered Egyptian forces to retake this land. Israel won the war that followed. But Sadat's actions made him very popular in Egypt and in other Arab countries.

Four years after the war, Sadat sought peace with Israel. He visited there to share his peace plan. Later he held peace talks in the United States with the Israeli prime minister, Menachem Begin. Because of their efforts, Sadat and Begin shared the 1978 Nobel Prize for Peace.

The following year, Egypt and Israel signed a peace treaty - Israel's first with an Arab country. Sadat's actions were praised around the world. But many Egyptians and other Arabs opposed the treaty. In 1981 Sadat was killed by religious **extremists** during a military parade.

LEARN MORE! READ THESE ARTICLES...
MENACHEM BEGIN (VOLUME 4) • EGYPT (VOLUME 8)
HASSAN FATHY (VOLUME 3)

DID YOU KNOW?
While Sadat was working to overthrow the Egyptian monarchy, he went to prison twice. The second time he was imprisoned, he taught himself French and English.

When Egypt and Israel were working to make peace, U.S. President Jimmy Carter was a great help. Here (from left to right) you see Sadat's wife, Jehan, and Sadat himself, with the U.S. first lady, Rosalynn Carter, and President Carter.
© Wally McNamee/Corbis

Answer: TRUE.

World Peacemaker

A peacemaker has to be impartial - that is, be fair and not take sides. U Thant was a true peacemaker. As the secretary-general of the United Nations between 1961 and 1971, he had the job of peacemaker among many warring countries.

U Thant was born in 1909 in Burma (now called Myanmar). 'U' is not a name but a term of respect similar to the English word 'Mister'. Thant means 'pure'. Thant was educated at the University of Rangoon. It was here that he met Thakin Nu, later called U Nu. U Nu went on to become the prime minister of Burma after World War II.

Nu recognized Thant's abilities and appointed him as a spokesman for the government. Later Thant became a **diplomat** when he was appointed a member of the Burmese representatives to the United Nations (UN). In 1957 he became his country's permanent representative to the UN, and he later served as vice president of the UN General Assembly.

When the UN's leader, the secretary-general, died in 1961, the United States and the Soviet Union could not agree on a new leader for the body. Though neither country got their first choice, they were able to settle on Thant as acceptable.

As secretary-general, Thant worked for peace around the world. In 1962 he aided in the removal of Soviet missiles from Cuba. He also helped to end the civil war in the Congo, and he established a peacekeeping force on Cyprus in the Mediterranean Sea. When India and Pakistan went to war in 1965, Thant flew to India to help negotiate the ceasefire.

LEARN MORE! READ THESE ARTICLES...
NELSON MANDELA (VOLUME 4) • YANGON (VOLUME 7)
MAO ZEDONG (VOLUME 4)

NELSON MANDELA (VOLUME 4) • YANGON (VOLUME 7)
MAO ZEDONG (VOLUME 4)

SEARCH LIGHT

True or false? U is U Thant's first name.

DID YOU KNOW?

In 1976 an island in New York's East River, near the UN headquarters, was decorated with trees and flowers and called U Thant.

U Thant was a faithful Buddhist, and he applied a Buddhist attitude of focus and open-mindedness to his work at the United Nations.
© Bettmann/Corbis

Answer: FALSE. U has a meaning similar to the word 'Mister'.

Men in Dragon Ships

'The Vikings are coming!'

When people in the seaside towns of northern Europe heard this cry, some of them prepared to fight. Others took their children, grabbed anything they could carry, and quickly fled. A thousand years ago, the arrival of Viking invaders in a coastal town caused great fear.

The Vikings were also called Norsemen (Northmen), because they came from Scandinavia - the area of northern Europe that includes the modern countries of Denmark, Norway, and Sweden. The Norsemen were **pagan** warriors who wanted adventure and treasures. Like pirates, they sailed around northern Europe, fighting, killing, and stealing in towns and villages.

Sometimes, the Vikings even took **captives** and sailed away with them. These captives had to serve their masters, but they often found that the Norsemen were not so fierce at home. When they weren't raiding other countries, many Norsemen were farmers.

The Vikings didn't always raid villages. Sometimes they traded with them. The Norsemen built special large boats called longships, or 'dragon ships', to carry goods to people in faraway lands. Vikings were brave sailors and would sometimes sail great distances with only the Sun, Moon, and stars to guide them.

In addition to pirating and trading, the Vikings also used their longships for exploring. It is believed that around the year AD 1000, a Viking called Leif Ericson sailed across the Atlantic Ocean and spent a winter in what is now Newfoundland, Canada. This would make him the first European to have landed in North America - about 500 years before Christopher Columbus!

LEARN MORE! READ THESE ARTICLES...
NORTH AMERICA (VOLUME 9) • NORWAY (VOLUME 6) • SHIPS (VOLUME 2)

Vikings were skilled sailors who used the position
of the Sun and the stars to find their way on the sea.
Their longships, made from the wood of oak trees,
carried their goods to foreign lands.
© Bettmann/Corbis

DID YOU KNOW?

A 'berserker' was a Viking warrior
who wrapped himself in bearskin (or
'bear shirt') and fought as if he
couldn't be harmed. Today, if someone
says you've 'gone berserk', they
mean that you're acting crazy.

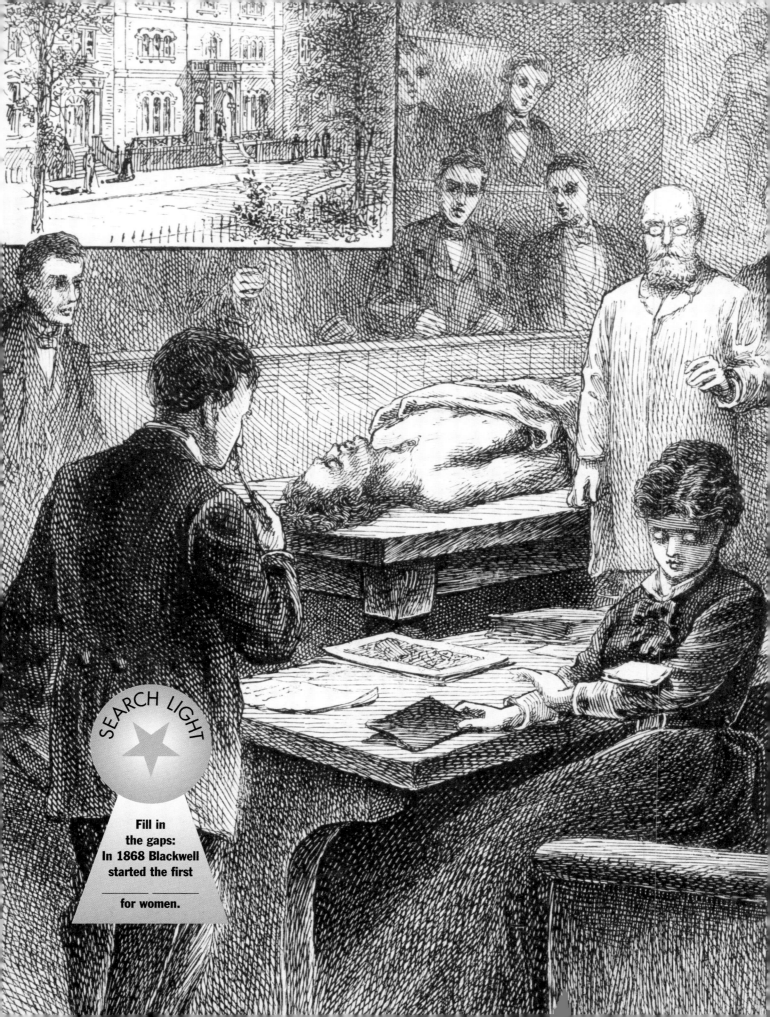

The First Modern Woman Doctor

Elizabeth Blackwell was born in England in 1821, but she moved to the United States with her family when she was 11. By the time she was 23, Blackwell had decided that she wanted to be a doctor. But at this time there were no female doctors in the United States.

It wasn't easy for Blackwell to study medicine. Most of the medical colleges she applied to turned her down. The men who taught medicine didn't think it was right for a woman to be a doctor. Finally Blackwell was admitted to Geneva Medical College in New York. She was the only woman in a class of 150.

The other medical students made things difficult for Blackwell. They criticized her, refused to talk to her, and kept her from taking part in the classroom medical demonstrations. However, two years later Blackwell was the best student in her class. In 1849 she became the first female doctor in the United States.

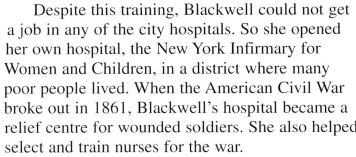

DID YOU KNOW?
A year after Blackwell opened her hospital, her sister Emily came to work with her. She, too, had become a doctor.

Photograph of Elizabeth Blackwell.
Courtesy, Hobart and William Smith Colleges

Despite this training, Blackwell could not get a job in any of the city hospitals. So she opened her own hospital, the New York Infirmary for Women and Children, in a district where many poor people lived. When the American Civil War broke out in 1861, Blackwell's hospital became a relief centre for wounded soldiers. She also helped select and train nurses for the war.

Blackwell worked to establish a medical school for women, so that other women could become doctors. In 1868 she opened the Woman's Medical College, the first of its kind in America.

LEARN MORE! READ THESE ARTICLES…
MARIE CURIE (VOLUME 4) • MEDICINE (VOLUME 2) • LOUIS PASTEUR (VOLUME 4)

Elizabeth Blackwell was not only the first American woman doctor. She also became the first woman to have her name placed on the British medical register. This meant she was allowed to practice medicine in Great Britain.
© Bettmann/Corbis

Answer: In 1868 Blackwell started the first medical school (or medical college) for women.

65

Inventing New Plants

Luther Burbank grew up on a farm in the United States. Although he went only to secondary school, he read Charles Darwin's ideas about how living things change over time. Burbank wanted to understand why different plants have different kinds of fruit and flowers and how they might be changed to grow better ones.

In the 1870s most people thought it wasn't possible to make new kinds of plants. But Burbank surprised them by creating hundreds of new varieties, including a white blackberry that was so clear, its seeds could be seen through its skin. Burbank grew a tomato on a potato vine and called it a 'pomato'. He combined a plum tree and an apricot tree to make a new fruit called a 'plumcot'.

Benefitting today from Burbank's work with plants.
© Lynda Richardson/Corbis

Burbank produced many plants by 'grafting'. He took a small twig from one plant and put it into a cut he made on a different plant. The plant with roots controlled the size of the new plant, while the twig grew into branches with flowers and fruit. Sometimes he produced completely new kinds of plants by cross-pollination. He did this by putting **pollen** from the flowers of one type of plant onto the sticky part of the flowers of another type of plant.

Getting the new plants he wanted was not easy. The white blackberry took Burbank 65,000 attempts to get it right. And he spent eight years cross-pollinating different types of daisy to turn a small yellowish daisy into a tall snow-white flower with a yellow centre. The result was the famous Shasta daisy.

Burbank's work produced many useful plants. And his experiments added greatly to the understanding of how features pass from parents to offspring.

LEARN MORE! READ THESE ARTICLES...
CHARLES DARWIN (VOLUME 4) • FOSSILS (VOLUME 1)
ROSE (VOLUME 10)

SEARCH LIGHT

Find and correct the mistake in the following sentence: Rafting is a way of making a new plant by sticking a twig from one plant into a cut on another plant.

© Corbis

DID YOU KNOW?

Luther Burbank developed more than 220 new varieties of trees, vegetables, fruits, flowers, and grasses.

Answer: Grafting is a way of making a new plant by sticking a twig from one plant into a cut on another plant.

SEARCH LIGHT

Find and correct the error in the following sentence: Copernicus studied the skies and finally decided that the Sun circles the Earth.

Student of the Sky

Hundreds of years ago many people thought that the Earth stayed still and the Sun went around it. Then came a man named Nicolaus Copernicus, who said that it was the Sun that stayed still and the Earth that moved. And he was mostly right.

Copernicus was born on 19 February 1473 in Poland. His father died a few years after Copernicus was born, and a wealthy uncle brought the young boy up. He sent him to the University of Kraków to study mathematics. There Copernicus also studied the stars and planets.

Copernicus didn't believe that the Earth was the centre of the universe and that all the other planets and stars circled around it. He studied the sky for years and finally decided that the Sun sat at the centre of the universe. The Earth and the other planets spun around the Sun.

DID YOU KNOW? Andreas Osiander, who was in charge of getting Copernicus' last book printed, made some changes and added a note to the front saying that the book wasn't meant to be true— all without the author's permission!

An image of the solar system as Copernicus imagined it.
© Stefano Bianchetti/Corbis

Some of what Copernicus said wasn't correct. We know today that all the planets and the stars, including the Sun, move constantly. We also know that the Sun is the centre not of the universe but rather of the solar system. Yet Copernicus was right in some ways. It is true that the Earth circles the Sun.

Copernicus presented his ideas in a book called *On the Revolutions of the Celestial Spheres*. The book wasn't published for 13 years because the Roman Catholic church opposed it. It is said that Copernicus received the first copy as he was dying - on 24 May 1543.

LEARN MORE! READ THESE ARTICLES…
ASTRONOMY (VOLUME 2) • GALILEO (VOLUME 4)
JOHANNES KEPLER (VOLUME 4)

Unlike most people in his day, Nicolaus Copernicus didn't believe that the Earth was the centre of the universe. And his studies eventually showed that he was right.
© Bettmann/Corbis

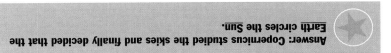

Answer: Copernicus studied the skies and finally decided that the Earth circles the Sun.

DID YOU KNOW?
Not only did Marie Curie win the Nobel Prize twice, but her daughter and son-in-law, Irène and Frédéric Joliot-Curie, shared the Nobel Prize in 1935.

Discovering a New Kind of Science

The French scientist Marie Curie became the first woman to win the Nobel Prize - one of the greatest honours in the world. What's more, she was the first person ever to win the prize twice.

SEARCH LIGHT

True or false? Marie Curie's research led to her death.

Marie Curie was born in Poland. She moved to France and studied at the great university known as the Sorbonne. She was one of the best students there. She worked very hard - often late into the night, sometimes eating little more than bread, butter, and tea.

She married Pierre Curie after completing her science and maths degree. Pierre was also a scientist, and the two worked together. Another scientist, named Henri Becquerel, had already discovered that certain types of material send out tiny 'bullets' of energy all the time. Marie Curie called this action 'radioactivity'.

These strange radioactive **particles** were far too small to be seen, but it was possible to take a kind of photograph of them. Marie Curie studied radioactivity and discovered two new **elements** that were radioactive: polonium and radium.

Over the years, Marie Curie's discoveries about radioactivity have proved extremely important in many ways. Radioactivity helps doctors identify and treat diseases. A major form of power generation based on nuclear energy has been developed, a process involving radioactivity. And in geology, radioactivity is used to determine the age of ancient rocks.

Marie Curie's entire life was spent working for science. She fell ill and eventually died because of working so closely with radioactive materials. She knew about the risk, but she felt her work was too important to stop. Marie Curie was awarded the Nobel Prize in 1903 for her work on radioactivity and in 1911 for discovering radium.

LEARN MORE! READ THESE ARTICLES...
ATOMS (VOLUME 2) • ELIZABETH BLACKWELL (VOLUME 4)
NUCLEAR ENERGY (VOLUME 2)

Answer: TRUE. Marie Curie's work with radioactive materials damaged her blood and caused her death.

DID YOU KNOW?
A skull that may be from one of our earliest human ancestors was recently found in the Sahel region of Africa. The skull is between 6 million and 7 million years old, more than a million years older than any skulls found before.

The Theory of Evolution

All cultures tell a story about how life on Earth began. Most traditions and religions say that creation happened in a particular event. But what does science tell us? A scientist named Charles Darwin came up with a very different idea about the origin of humans and other creatures.

Darwin and his ideas being made fun of in a magazine.
© Archivo Iconografico S.A./Corbis

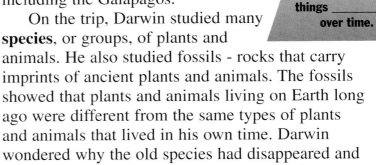

Fill in the gap: Darwin's theory of evolution says that species of living things _____ over time.

In 1831, at the age of 22, Darwin set out from England on a scientific expedition aboard a ship called the *Beagle*. He sailed to the coast of South America and the Pacific islands, including the Galapagos.

On the trip, Darwin studied many **species**, or groups, of plants and animals. He also studied fossils - rocks that carry imprints of ancient plants and animals. The fossils showed that plants and animals living on Earth long ago were different from the same types of plants and animals that lived in his own time. Darwin wondered why the old species had disappeared and the new species had developed.

After much thought, this is what Darwin decided. Living things must work hard for food and shelter, so only the ones that do this best will survive. Small individual strengths, such as being bigger or faster, can be the key to survival. And these strengths are passed on to the individuals' offspring. Helpful individual differences add up over time to make the whole species change, or evolve.

This was Darwin's famous **theory** of **evolution**. He also believed that, over time, the same species living in different surroundings could evolve into two separate species.

Darwin published his theory in his books *On the Origin of Species* and *The Descent of Man*. He proposed that all living things, including humans, have slowly evolved from earlier species. Many people do not accept Darwin's theory. But it is still the most widely accepted scientific theory.

LEARN MORE! READ THESE ARTICLES...
LUTHER BURBANK (VOLUME 4) • FOSSILS (VOLUME 1) • GALAPAGOS ISLANDS (VOLUME 9)

Answer: Darwin's theory of evolution says that species of living things change (or evolve) over time.

A Brilliant Wonderer

Young Albert Einstein didn't always do well in school in Germany. His teachers thought he took too long to answer questions. And often they got upset because Albert thought of questions they couldn't answer.

The Einstein Memorial, a sculpture in honour of the great scientist, in Washington, D.C., U.S.
© Roman Soumar/Corbis

The more Albert learned, the more things he thought about. The more he thought, the more questions he had. By age 12 he had decided that he would solve the riddle of the 'huge world' - the universe.

Einstein thought there must be some rules to explain why everything in the universe, big and little, acts as it does. How can gravity attract distant objects through empty space? What makes tiny atoms stick together to form all the different things there are?

He thought and thought until he believed he had some of the answers for things that scientists had long tried to work out - such as what makes gravity work and how fast light can travel. Einstein even proved such unexpected things as the fact that light bends under the force of gravity.

You may have heard of Einstein's famous formula $E = mc^2$. This stands for a complex idea called 'relativity'. But in the simplest terms it shows that a small **particle** of matter is equal to an enormous quantity of energy.

Einstein introduced entirely new ways of thinking about time, space, matter, energy, and gravity. His ideas guided such scientific advances as space exploration and the control of atomic energy. One of the concepts he explained, the **photoelectric effect**, led to something most people enjoy daily: television.

SEARCH LIGHT

Find and correct the error in the following sentence: Albert Einstein invented gravity.

LEARN MORE! READ THESE ARTICLES...
ATOMS (VOLUME 2) • NUCLEAR ENERGY (VOLUME 2)
UNIVERSE (VOLUME 2)

DID YOU KNOW?
One story about Einstein has it that he once used a check for $1,500 as a bookmark - and lost it.

Albert Einstein, shown here in his study, introduced entirely new ways of thinking about time, space, matter, energy, and gravity.
© Bettmann/Corbis

Answer: Albert Einstein explained gravity.

This fresco (a painting created on wet plaster) shows
Galileo demonstrating his version of the telescope.
© Archivo Iconografico, S.A./Corbis

DID YOU KNOW?
Galileo agreed with Nicolaus
Copernicus and Johannes Kepler
that the Earth orbits the Sun. This
upset the Roman Catholic church,
and Galileo was forced to tell
everyone he was wrong.

The Man Who Discovered Outer Space

Galileo Galilei was born in Pisa, Italy, in 1564. As a young man he became interested in mathematics and **astronomy**. He loved to experiment and try out new ideas.

A story claims that Galileo once dropped objects of different weights from the top of the famous Leaning Tower of Pisa. He wanted to prove that things fall at the same speed, no matter how much they weigh. But some of Galileo's ideas angered other scientists, so he left Pisa and went to Padua.

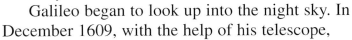

Galileo.
© Bettmann/Corbis

For years Galileo taught mathematics at the University of Padua. But in 1609 his career changed direction. Galileo heard about the telescope, a Dutch invention that could make distant objects appear closer. Galileo figured out how such a device would work and then used **lenses** from spectacle makers' shops to make his own telescopes. Galileo's telescopes were better than most and could make objects appear up to 20 times larger than what the naked eye could see.

Galileo began to look up into the night sky. In December 1609, with the help of his telescope, Galileo learned that the Moon's surface is rough and uneven. A month later he discovered four moons orbiting the planet Jupiter. Also, when Galileo studied Saturn, he noticed something mysterious about its appearance. Later scientists would learn that the planet's strange look was due to its large rings.

Using his telescopes, Galileo helped change how people looked up at space. Likewise, much of the modern science of **physics** is based on his ideas - especially his ideas about how objects of all sizes move and how helpful it is to test scientific ideas by experimenting.

LEARN MORE! READ THESE ARTICLES...
ASTRONOMY (VOLUME 2)
NICOLAUS COPERNICUS (VOLUME 4) • ITALY (VOLUME 6)

SEARCH LIGHT

Fill in the gap: Galileo built his own _____, which was an improvement on others built earlier.

Answer: Galileo built his own telescope, which was an improvement on others built earlier.

77

The Woman Who Lived with Chimpanzees

In the 1940s a young English girl named Jane Goodall dreamed of living in the African forests among the animals she'd read about. As she grew older, Goodall began to make her dream come true.

Jane Goodall presenting a stuffed toy monkey to United Nations Secretary-General Kofi Annan in 2002.
© AFP/Corbis

In 1957, when she was about 23 years old, a school friend invited Goodall to Kenya, in Africa. While in Africa, Goodall met the famous scientist Dr Louis Leakey. At the time, Leakey was studying wild chimpanzees in order to find out more about the origins of human life. He was impressed by Goodall's interest in animals and encouraged her to study chimpanzees in Tanzania.

Some people thought that Goodall wouldn't last for more than a few months in the forest amongst the wild animals. But Goodall proved them wrong and ended up living in Tanzania for 15 years. During that time, the chimpanzees slowly became used to Goodall and finally allowed her to spend hours around them.

Being able to watch the chimpanzees up close allowed Goodall to discover many things about the animals that people did not know. Goodall saw chimpanzees use sticks as simple tools to draw termites and ants out of their nests. Goodall also found that all chimpanzees are different from each other in their behaviour and **natures**, just like people.

As a child, Jane Goodall grew up reading about wild animals. But as an adult, she ended up writing many books of her own. In them she shared what she learned from 15 years of living with the wild chimpanzees of Africa.

DID YOU KNOW?
Before Goodall's studies, scientists believed chimpanzees were vegetarians. But Goodall learned that they do sometimes hunt and eat meat.

LEARN MORE! READ THESE ARTICLES...
AFRICA (VOLUME 8) • APES (VOLUME 12)
CHARLES DARWIN (VOLUME 4)

Jane Goodall spent many years in Africa studying chimpanzees. She encountered this curious chimp at the Gombe Stream Research Center in Tanzania in 1972.
© Bettmann/Corbis

SEARCH LIGHT

Jane Goodall liked to read about Tarzan, Mowgli, and Dr Dolittle. What do all three storybook characters have in common?

Answer: Tarzan, Mowgli, and Dr Dolittle all lived with animals.

DID YOU KNOW?
Kepler's grave was lost during a war, but the words he composed for his gravestone still survive:
I used to measure the heavens,
now I shall measure the shadows of the earth.
Although my soul was from heaven,
the shadow of my body lies here.

Stargazer

Johannes Kepler was born on 27 December 1571 in Germany. He was to grow up to be an important astronomer who made many discoveries about the stars. Astronomers study the movements of planets, stars, comets, and meteors. However, for most of his life Kepler studied and taught mathematics.

When he was 23 years old, Kepler became an official calendar maker. Calendar making was a difficult job because certain church holy days had to happen just as a particular star was in a particular spot in the sky. It took a lot of complicated maths to make a good calendar.

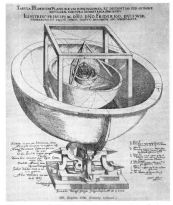

Diagram of Kepler's first model of the universe.
© Bettmann/Corbis

In 1597 Kepler published his first important work, *The Cosmographic Mystery*. Kepler's book explained the distance of the planets from the Sun. Kepler also said that all the planets revolve around the Sun and that the Sun remains in one position - an idea that built on those of the earlier astronomer Nicolaus Copernicus.

In 1600 Kepler moved to Prague, where he soon became Emperor Rudolf II's **imperial** mathematician, the most important mathematics post in Europe. Kepler discovered that Mars's orbit is an ellipse (an oval-like shape) rather than a circle. He also explained important laws for the motion of all of the planets around the Sun.

Kepler's scientific work focused on astronomy. But he also studied other sciences and mathematics so he could learn everything possible about the stars.

LEARN MORE! READ THESE ARTICLES...
CALENDAR (VOLUME 2) • NICOLAUS COPERNICUS (VOLUME 4)
GALILEO (VOLUME 4)

SEARCH LIGHT

Kepler was a teacher of
a) science.
b) German.
c) maths.
d) astronomy.

Johannes Kepler became the official mathematician to Emperor Rudolf II. This picture shows him explaining some of his discoveries to the emperor.
© Bettmann/Corbis

Answer: c) maths.

DID YOU KNOW?
The story of Newton and the apple isn't true, but it is a good way to remember something important about someone famous.

An Apple, an Idea

When you throw a ball into the air, do you wonder why it always comes back down? Why doesn't it keep going up?

One man did more than wonder. He was Sir Isaac Newton.

There is a story that says Newton was sitting under an apple tree when an apple struck him on the head. He wondered why the apple fell down instead of up. Was there a force that no one could see, pulling the apple to the ground?

Newton's reflecting telescope, made in 1668.
© James A. Sugar/Corbis

Actually, it was Newton's observation of the motions of the planets that contributed most importantly to his great discovery: the *Law of Universal Gravitation*. This 'natural law' helps explain why the Earth, the Moon, and the planets don't bump into each other. It explains why things feel light or heavy and what makes them fall to the ground.

What Newton decided was that everything has gravity. And every object's gravity has a pull on everything else around it. Heavy things pull harder than light ones.

Newton worked out many other things too. Did you know that white light is actually made of seven colours? These are the colours that make up a rainbow. Newton discovered this. He let the light pass through a **prism**, and the seven colours all came through separately. He then let the colours pass through another prism and they combined back into white light.

Newton's investigations also led him to invent the first reflecting telescope, which uses mirrors to gather light to improve a telescope's capability. His design is still used by amateur telescope makers.

Isaac Newton was one of the greatest scientists who ever lived. He died in 1727 and was buried in Westminster Abbey in London, England. He was the first scientist to be honoured in this way.

LEARN MORE! READ THESE ARTICLES…
GRAVITY (VOLUME 2) • RAINBOWS (VOLUME 1) • TELESCOPES (VOLUME 2)

SEARCH LIGHT

Find and correct the mistake in the following sentence: Newton's *Theory of Reflecting Telescopes* helped explain why the planets don't bump into each other.

Sir Isaac Newton's theory of gravity contributed to his lasting reputation as one of the greatest scientists of all time.
© Bettmann/Corbis

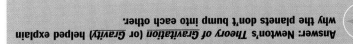

DID YOU KNOW?
In 1868 Pasteur saved the French silk industry. Silk businesses were facing ruin because of a mysterious disease that attacked the silkworms. Pasteur worked out a way of detecting the disease and preventing it from spreading.

The Man Who Conquered Disease

In the 1800s, the bite of a dog with rabies meant certain death for the person who had been bitten. In 1885, when a rabid dog bit a boy called Joseph Meister, his mother was desperate. She went to the only man she thought might be able to cure her son.

Pasteur had found that rabies was caused by a virus - a disease-causing **agent** so small it could not be seen, even under a microscope. He had already worked out a way to defeat the rabies virus in animals. But he had never tried his treatment on humans. Pasteur treated Joseph, and Joseph became the first person to be cured of rabies.

Pasteur devoted his life to solving the problems of industry, farming, and medicine. He discovered that if a liquid like milk is heated to a certain temperature for a few minutes, it takes longer to spoil. If milk is not treated in this way, tiny living organisms called 'bacteria' cause it to go bad. These organisms are killed by heat in a process that came to be called 'pasteurization'.

Pasteur also discovered that many diseases are caused by germs that enter the body from outside. In 1877 he tried to find a cure for anthrax, a disease that affects the lungs and kills cattle and sheep. Pasteur successfully developed the method known as 'immunization'. Immunization means giving a patient a weak dose of a virus that the patient can fight off. Then the patient's body knows how to stop an actual case of the disease.

SEARCH LIGHT

Pasteurization refers to
a) a disease-causing organism.
b) a weak dose of a disease.
c) heating something to kill bacteria.

Scientist Louis Pasteur.
© Hulton-Deutsch Collection/Corbis

LEARN MORE! READ THESE ARTICLES...
ELIZABETH BLACKWELL (VOLUME 4) • MARIE CURIE (VOLUME 4)
MEDICINE (VOLUME 2)

Louis Pasteur's discoveries are among the most important in the history of medical science. He is often known as the founder of microbiology - the study of simple life forms too small to be seen with the naked eye.
© Hulton-Deutsch Collection/Corbis

When gold was discovered near the Cherokee Indian territory in Georgia, the U.S. government drove the Native Americans from their land to new territory. Here, Cherokee dancers perform at a modern gathering that preserves Indian traditions, the Chehaw National Indian Festival in Albany, Georgia.

© Kevin Fleming/Corbis

SEARCH LIGHT

Which Native American Indian group used adobe to build houses?
a) Plains Indians
b) Pueblo Indians
c) Northwest Coast Indians

The First Native North Americans

The original peoples of North America are called Indians, American Indians, Native Americans, or (in Canada) First Nations. They lived in America long before Europeans arrived. Many North American places are known by their Indian names - including Massachusetts, Lake Huron, and the Mississippi River in the United States and Ottawa, Ontario, and Saskatchewan in Canada.

(Left) American Indian children in traditional dress.
(Right) Portrait of Cherokee warrior Austenaco.

Each group of American Indians lived differently, depending on the land around them. Eastern America had many lakes, rivers, and vast forests. The Indians there lived in villages, often in wooden houses. The men were hunters and the women were farmers.

In the West, the Plains Indians lived on large rolling areas of grassland. Bison (sometimes called 'buffalo') wandered the plains in large herds, and hunting them gave the Indians everything they needed to survive. These Indians didn't stay in one place but followed the bison's **migration**.

The Southwestern states were dry and mountainous. The Pueblo Indians were farmers and lived in stone and adobe (sun-dried clay) houses. They also built cave houses on the sides of cliffs, high on the faces of **mesas**.

The Northwest Indians lived along the northern coast of the Pacific Ocean and fished in the ocean and rivers. They created tall, painted totem poles showing important animals and ancestors.

When Europeans arrived in the Americas, they wanted the land. They often **betrayed** and attacked the Indians and stole their lands. Many U.S. and Canadian **descendants** of the original Native American Indians have long lived on reservations - areas put aside by the government. But this has tended to cut them off from others, weaken their traditions, and limit their rights. Today Indians must work hard to keep their ancient culture and customs alive.

LEARN MORE! READ THESE ARTICLES...
A CHEROKEE STORY: WHY POSSUM'S TAIL IS BARE (VOLUME 5)
MAYAN CIVILIZATION (VOLUME 9) • ONTARIO, CANADA (VOLUME 9)

Answer: b) Pueblo Indians

DID YOU KNOW?
The money in Venezuela is named for the South American liberator Simón Bolívar. It's called the *bolívar*.

Hero of Many Nations

In the early 1800s, in the country that would become Venezuela, there lived a man with a big dream. He wanted the countries of Spanish South America to become independent from Spain and join together as one strong country.

This man was Simón Bolívar. For years he fought the Spanish in support of this dream, and many people came to help him from all over the world. Many of them sailed from Europe and searched all over South America to find him.

Bolívar was born in 1783. His **liberation** of New Granada - now Colombia, Ecuador, and parts of several other countries - is one of the most daring acts in the history of war. In the spring of 1819 he led a small army of 2,500 men through floodwaters and across icy mountain passes, through places where there were no paths at all. Tired and hungry, they finally arrived in Boyacá, near Bogotá, the capital of New Granada. There they surprised a big Spanish army. Fighting fiercely, they beat the Spanish and freed New Granada.

Portrait of Simón Bolívar by M.N. Bate.
© Bettmann/Corbis

Bolívar fought many battles to free other countries in South America, including his native Venezuela. His dream of freeing the South American countries from Spain came true. But even if he was never able to join all the different countries together as one nation, he is one of the most important heroes in South America. The South American country of Bolivia was named in his honour.

LEARN MORE! READ THESE ARTICLES...
FIDEL CASTRO (VOLUME 4) • COLOMBIA (VOLUME 9) • SOUTH AMERICA (VOLUME 9)

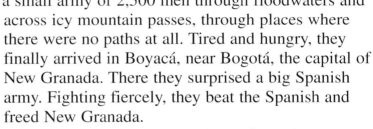

SEARCH LIGHT

True or false? Bolívar made all of South America come together as one nation.

In addition to the countries that are now Colombia and Ecuador, Simón Bolívar and his troops won the independence of Venezuela and Peru.
© Bettmann/Corbis

Answer: FALSE. He did, however, help free many nations from Spanish rule.

DID YOU KNOW?

A new English translation of Anne Frank's diary was published in 1995. The new edition has material that was not in the original version and is nearly one-third longer.

SEARCH LIGHT

True or false? Anne Frank went on to write many other famous books.

A Young Girl and Her Diary

During World War II in Europe, the Nazis of Germany tried to destroy the Jewish people and their culture. The Nazis had taken control of many countries, including the Netherlands (Holland). In the city of Amsterdam, the Nazi threat forced a young Jewish girl and her family to spend two years in hiding. Anne Frank's moving diary of those years in hiding has since become a classic book.

Anne Frank.
Anne Frank House, Amsterdam and Anne Frank-Fonds, Basel—Hulton/Archive by Getty Images

Halfway through the war, the Nazis began sending Jews to prison camps. So in July 1942, Anne's family went into hiding in the back-room office and warehouse of Anne's father's business. Four other Jews hid with them in the small space, and non-Jewish friends smuggled food and other supplies to them.

Anne was 13 when she went into hiding. In her diary, she describes daily life in the secret rooms. She also writes about her own dreams and feelings while growing up in hiding.

The family never once left their hideout until the Nazi police discovered them in August 1944. Then the Frank family was moved to the concentration camp at Auschwitz in Poland, where Anne's mother died in 1945. Anne and her sister were sent to another camp, Bergen-Belsen, where they both died of typhus. Anne's father, Otto Frank, was the only family member who survived.

Friends had found Anne's diary in the hiding space. After the war, they gave it to her father, and he published it in 1947. Since then, Anne's story of courage and hope has inspired millions of readers. Today, the Frank family's hiding place in Amsterdam is a museum.

LEARN MORE! READ THESE ARTICLES...
AMSTERDAM, NETHERLANDS (VOLUME 6) • GERMANY (VOLUME 6)
JUDAISM (VOLUME 5)

Anne Frank sits at her desk at school in 1940.
She left school at the age of 13 to go into hiding.
Anne Frank House, Amsterdam and Anne Frank-Fonds, Basel—Hulton/Archive by Getty Images

Answer: FALSE. Anne died during World War II, and her diary is the only writing of hers that survived.

Gold Medallist in Athletics

When she won the 400-metre world championship in 1997, Cathy Freeman ran a victory lap carrying two flags. One was the flag of her country, Australia. The other was that of her people, the Aboriginals. The Aboriginals are the original people of Australia, who have suffered great mistreatment and injustice since the Europeans came to their country. Her choice to carry both flags was **controversial**. But it showed Freeman's strong sense of national and ethnic pride.

Cathy Freeman holding the Olympic torch in 2000.
© Reuters NewMedia Inc./Corbis

While Freeman was growing up in Queensland, her father encouraged her to start running. By the time she was 17, Freeman had won a gold medal at the 1990 Commonwealth Games and been named Young Australian of the Year. In 1992 she was the first Australian Aboriginal woman to compete in the Olympic Games.

At the 1994 Commonwealth Games, Freeman took home gold medals in the 400-metre and 200-metre races. Her win in the 200-metre race set a national record. Perhaps Freeman's greatest race was at the 1996 Olympic Games in Atlanta, Georgia, U.S. She ran against the world record holder, Marie-José Pérec of France. The two champions raced neck and neck. Finally, it was Pérec who shot ahead to the finish line.

In 1997 Freeman was named Australian of the Year. A year later, however, she injured her foot and had to withdraw from the Commonwealth Games. Freeman didn't let the injury stop her, and in 1999 she was running again. She came back and successfully defended her 400-metre world championship title. At the Sydney Olympics in 2000, Freeman had the great honour of lighting the Olympic torch. A week later her dream of Olympic gold came true when she won the 400-metre race in front of her fellow Australians. Again she took her victory lap proudly carrying both the Australian and Aboriginal flags.

LEARN MORE! READ THESE ARTICLES...
AUSTRALIA (VOLUME 7) • PELÉ (VOLUME 4) • KATH WALKER (VOLUME 3)

Cathy Freeman was the first Aboriginal to win an individual medal in an Olympic event. She won the 400-metre race at the 2000 Olympics in Sydney, Australia.
© Duomo/Corbis

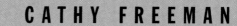

DID YOU KNOW?
In a rush to get to her first track race, 8-year-old Cathy Freeman ran into a post and hurt her eye. She ran her first race with one eye closed and won it easily.

Salt and Empires

In March of 1930, a 61-year-old Indian man started out on a long walk to the ocean. When people asked where he was going, Mohandas ('Mahatma') Gandhi replied, 'I am going to the ocean to get some salt.' Soon thousands joined him in a trip that lasted a month and became known as the 'Salt March'.

Mohandas K. Gandhi was a Hindu Indian who had studied law in London. India was controlled by Britain, and when Gandhi returned home he was angered by the poverty and inequality he saw in his country. Rather than fight the British with guns or bombs,

Mahatma Gandhi.
© Bettmann/Corbis

Gandhi believed in simply refusing to obey unjust laws. For example, he urged Indians to make their own clothing so they wouldn't have to buy British goods. Hindus began to call Gandhi 'Mahatma', which means 'great soul'.

Most Indians could not afford to buy expensive British salt, but it was against the law for them to make their own. So Gandhi walked 300 kilometres to the sea to make salt from seawater. After the Salt March, the British put Gandhi in jail. It wasn't the first or the last time he was jailed for leading non-violent protests. Gandhi went to jail cheerfully. When he came out, he went back to teaching Indians how to regain control of their country by peaceful means. India finally won independence from Britain in 1947.

After India became independent, there was violence between the country's Hindu and Muslim populations. During the last year of his life, Gandhi worked to build peace between all the peoples of India.

LEARN MORE! READ THESE ARTICLES...
INDIA (VOLUME 7) • MARTIN LUTHER KING JR (VOLUME 4)
RABINDRANATH TAGORE (VOLUME 3)

Mahatma Gandhi, leader of the Indian non-violent protest, marches with supporters to the shore at Dandi to collect salt in violation of the law. Following this action, he was jailed.
© Bettmann/Corbis

Answer: FALSE. Mohandas was his name. Mahatma was a title of respect.

95

True or false? Helen Keller was born deaf and blind.

Helen Keller (on the left) is shown here reading the lips of her teacher, Anne Sullivan (on the right). Sullivan stayed with her pupil from 1887 until her own death in 1936.
© Corbis

Woman of Courage

Helen Keller became blind and deaf soon after she was born, but she still managed to learn to read, write, and speak.

Helen was born in Alabama in the United States in 1880. At 19 months old she fell ill, probably with scarlet fever. She recovered but lost her eyesight and hearing. Since she couldn't hear other people, she didn't learn to speak.

Helen Keller in her later years.
EB Inc.

When Helen was 6 years old, Alexander Graham Bell examined her. He was a doctor for speech correction as well as being the inventor of the telephone. Bell sent a special teacher, Anne Sullivan, to stay with Helen as her **governess**.

Sullivan was herself a remarkable woman. She was very patient and taught Helen that things had names. She taught Helen to finger spell the alphabet. By using finger spelling on Helen's palm, Sullivan helped Helen understand names for things that she could feel.

Helen was a hard worker and soon learned to read a form of the alphabet with her fingers. She started to read by feeling raised letters and words on cardboard. Later she learned **Braille**, a system of writing that many blind people use. Another teacher, Sarah Fuller, taught Helen to speak by having her feel people's lips and throats as they were talking.

Despite her blindness, Helen Keller wrote numerous articles and several books, including *The Story of My Life* and *Helen Keller's Journal*. Her early life with Anne Sullivan is the subject of a well-known play and film called *The Miracle Worker*.

Helen Keller died when she was 88 years old. She is remembered as a woman of great courage and intelligence.

LEARN MORE! READ THESE ARTICLES...
ELIZABETH BLACKWELL (VOLUME 4)
BRAILLE (VOLUME 2) • SIGHT AND SOUND (VOLUME 2)

DID YOU KNOW?
As an adult, Helen Keller lectured all over the world. And her efforts to improve the treatment of deaf and blind people helped to stop the practice of putting people with physical disabilities into asylums for the mentally ill.

Answer: FALSE. Helen Keller became deaf and blind after an illness when she was almost 2 years old.

Civil Rights Leader

On 1 December 1955, in Montgomery, Alabama, U.S., a black woman called Rosa Parks was arrested. She had refused to give up her seat on a bus to a white man. At that time, the law said that black people had to sit only in certain sections of trains and buses

Martin Luther King Jr riding a bus in Montgomery, Alabama, U.S., in 1956.
© Bettmann/Corbis

and use different public toilets and even drinking fountains from the ones white people used. Rosa Parks's action sparked protests by black residents of the city. And Martin Luther King Jr was chosen to lead the protests.

King was a Baptist minister and a student of the Indian leader Mahatma Gandhi. He believed that non-violence was the most powerful way for people to make their point. This means demanding rights through peaceful methods, such as **strikes** and protests, not by fighting. The protests he led became known as the Montgomery bus **boycott**. The law was changed after a year of protests.

However, black people still didn't receive the same rights and privileges as white people. In 1963 King and his supporters were imprisoned because of their protests against **discrimination**. When he was freed, King and other **civil rights** leaders organized a march on Washington, D.C., the national capital. There, King delivered a powerful speech to hundreds of thousands of people, saying: 'I have a dream.' His dream was that one day all people would be equal, like brothers.

For his work on civil rights, King was awarded the Nobel Prize for Peace in 1964. Through all his struggles, King used only peaceful methods of protest. But in April 1968, King was shot dead in Memphis, Tennessee, by James Earl Ray.

LEARN MORE! READ THESE ARTICLES...
GWENDOLYN BROOKS (VOLUME 3) • NELSON MANDELA (VOLUME 4)
UNITED STATES: A YOUNG AND POWERFUL NATION (VOLUME 9)

SEARCH LIGHT

True or false? Martin Luther King Jr set off the Montgomery bus boycott.

Martin Luther King Jr led the march on Washington in 1963. His protests helped win important rights for African Americans.

DID YOU KNOW?

In 1977, King was posthumously (after his death) awarded the Presidential Medal of Freedom. This is the U.S. government's highest honour awarded to a person not in the military.

Answer: FALSE. Rosa Parks set off the boycott when she refused to give up her seat.

Around-the-World Voyager

Hundreds of years ago, only very brave men took the risk of travelling the open seas to reach unknown lands. Ferdinand Magellan was one such man.

Magellan was born into a **noble** family in Portugal in about 1480. When he was about 25, he joined the Portuguese navy, where he fought in numerous battles and saw many new places. But the king of Portugal refused to increase his **wages** after a decade of service, so Magellan went to work for the Spanish king.

An illustration of Ferdinand Magellan's ship Victoria.
Collection of the Bibliotheque Nationale; photo, © Erich Lessing/Art Resource, New York

At that time, Portugal controlled the sea route around Africa to the Indian Ocean to reach the rich Spice Islands (now called the East Indies). Magellan decided to sail west to find a new route to the islands. He set out in 1519, sailing across the Atlantic and down the coast of South America. He hoped to discover a passage to the ocean beyond South America. When he found it, he named it the Strait of Magellan. The ocean on the other side appeared calm and peaceful. Magellan called it the Pacific, from the Latin word for 'peaceful'.

After 99 more days, Magellan's ship reached the island now known as Guam. Landing in the islands we call the Philippines, Magellan and his men fought with islanders. Magellan was killed there on 27 April 1521.

A crewman, Juan Sebastián de Elcano, took command. The remaining crew sailed to the Spice Islands, loaded up with spices, and returned to Spain. In a voyage that took more than three years, they became the first men to circle the globe. But during that time, 200 men had died.

SEARCH LIGHT

Unscramble the following words:
- utgroPal
- ciSpe sladIns
- fiPicac nOace

LEARN MORE! READ THESE ARTICLES…
PACIFIC OCEAN (VOLUME 1) • PHILIPPINES (VOLUME 7) • PORTUGAL (VOLUME 6)

This painting from 1970 shows the Portuguese explorer Ferdinand Magellan. He led an expedition that was the first to travel all the way around the Earth.
The Art Archive/Marine Museum, Lisbon/Dagli Orti

**Answer: utgroPal = Portugal
ciSpe sladIns = Spice Islands
fiPicac nOace = Pacific Ocean**

Writers, Mathematicians, and Architects

Thousands of years ago there were people who built huge pyramids and temples. They had accurate calendars, did complex mathematics, and developed a writing system. They weren't the Egyptians, however. They were the Maya. They were the only Central Americans of their time to develop writing.

Temple of the Giant Jaguar at Tikal, Guatemala.
© Jan Butchofsky-Houser/Corbis

Mayan **culture** grew up in a region of Mexico and Central America called Mesoamerica. This includes the Yucatán Peninsula, parts of southern Mexico, Guatemala, Belize, and western Honduras and El Salvador.

Between about AD 200 and 900, the Maya built religious centres and cities from the jungles of Guatemala to the dry northern Yucatán in Mexico. These included Tikal, Uaxactún, and Palenque. The cities had populations of 5,000 to 50,000 people.

The Maya worshipped several gods and even offered human **sacrifices**. Many of their buildings are decorated with the face of Chac, the rain god. He was an important god in their farming society. Mayan rulers were considered to be the **descendants** of gods.

Most of the Maya were maize farmers. The upper classes were artists, writers, and **architects**. They developed a hieroglyphic (picture-based) writing system and a 365-day **solar** calendar. They were good **astronomers**, charting the movements of the planets through the night sky.

No one knows why Mayan culture faded. The cities began emptying after AD 900, and they were entirely empty by the time the Spaniards arrived in the 16th century. They stood overgrown by jungle until they were rediscovered in the 19th century. The decline may have been because of overuse of their farmland, overpopulation, climate changes, disease, or war - or a combination of these things.

LEARN MORE! READ THESE ARTICLES…
AMERICAN INDIANS (VOLUME 4) • CENTRAL AMERICA (VOLUME 9)
MEXICO (VOLUME 9)

DID YOU KNOW?
Today many Maya Indians live in northern Yucatán, Mexico, and the highlands of Guatemala, just as their ancestors did.

The Mayan civilization had more than 40 cities at the height of its power. Those cities were all abandoned by the early 16th century. Their remains can be seen in the jungles of Guatemala.
© Charles and Josette Lenars/Corbis

SEARCH LIGHT

Why did the ancient Mayan civilization fade?

Answer: No one is really sure. However, it may have been because of overuse of farmland, overpopulation, climate changes, disease, or war - or perhaps a combination of these.

Football Star

SEARCH LIGHT

Pelé played
for which
country?
a) Brazil
b) Peru
c) Colombia

One man, more than any other, has helped to make football (soccer) popular around the world. That man is Pelé. Pelé, whose real name is Edson Arantes do Nascimento, was born in 1940 in Brazil.

Pelé made his **debut** with the Santos Football Club in 1956. With Pelé playing forward, the team won several South American cups. In 1962 the team won its first world championship. Pelé also played for Brazil's national team and helped it to win the World Cup championship in 1958, 1962, and 1970.

Pelé holding international football award for 'Footballer of the Century'.
© AFP/Corbis

Pelé was a brilliant player who possessed great speed and balance. He could guess the moves of other players and had good control of the ball. In addition to all this, he could kick a ball powerfully with either foot, or direct it with his head, straight into the goal.

Pelé scored a career total of 1,281 goals in 1,363 matches, with 139 in one year alone. He scored his 1,000th goal in 1969. Pelé's career made him a national hero in Brazil. His fans call him Pérola Negra, meaning 'Black Pearl'.

Although Pelé retired in 1974, he made a comeback the following year with a New York team, the Cosmos. He said he returned to 'make soccer truly popular in the United States.' He succeeded, becoming a star in the United States as well.

Pelé's skills did not stop on the football field. He has also written best-selling **autobiographies**, starred in several films, and composed music, including the whole soundtrack for the 1977 film *Pelé*.

LEARN MORE! READ THESE ARTICLES...
BRAZIL (VOLUME 9) • CATHY FREEMAN (VOLUME 4) • TENZING NORGAY (VOLUME 4)

Pelé in action was so magical to watch that once two armies stopped fighting just to watch him play.
© AFP/Corbis

DID YOU KNOW?
When Pelé first went for trials with the major league football teams, he was repeatedly turned down.

Mother of the Poor and Dying

During her lifetime Mother Teresa became known worldwide for her kindness and her **charitable** work.

Mother Teresa was born Agnes Gonxha Bojaxhiu in Albania (now Macedonia) in 1910. When she was 18 years old, she decided to become a nun in the Roman Catholic church. She travelled to Ireland and there she joined the Institute of the Blessed Virgin Mary. She took **vows** promising to live a simple life and not to marry, and she became Sister Teresa.

The Institute had charity missions in India, and soon Sister Teresa sailed to the country to work as a teacher. Over the next 17 years, she taught in two schools in India, one of which was in Calcutta (now Kolkata). She saw firsthand the poverty and suffering of the people. She often said that she was inspired to make two important decisions in her life. One was to become a nun, and in 1946 the other was to devote her life to helping the sick and the poor.

As soon as her studies in nursing were finished, she began working with the people living in Calcutta's slums. She became an Indian citizen. And she became Mother Teresa when she founded the Missionaries of Charity. This was a new order of Roman Catholic nuns who wanted to help the sick, especially the dying and disabled.

Under Mother Teresa's guidance, the Missionaries of Charity opened centres all over the world. In these centres anyone could receive care, no matter what their religion. In 1979 Mother Teresa was awarded the Nobel Prize for Peace. Soon after her death, in 1997, the Roman Catholic church began the process to have Mother Teresa declared a saint.

SEARCH LIGHT

Was Mother Teresa Indian by birth?

LEARN MORE! READ THESE ARTICLES...
ELIZABETH BLACKWELL (VOLUME 4)
INDIA (VOLUME 7) • MEDICINE (VOLUME 2)

DID YOU KNOW?
When Mother Teresa founded her religious order, the Missionaries of Charity, her Indian nuns adopted the *sari* as their habit, or official dress. The *sari* is a garment worn by most women of India, Pakistan, and Bangladesh.

Mother Teresa lived in poverty with some of India's poorest people. She made it her life's work to care for the country's poor and dying.
© Bettmann/Corbis

Answer: No. Mother Teresa was born in Albania (now Macedonia), near Greece. But she lived and worked in India and became an Indian citizen.

107

On Top of the World

On 29 May 1953, at 11.30 AM, Tenzing Norgay and Edmund Hillary became the first people to reach the **summit** of the highest mountain on Earth, Mount Everest.

Tenzing Norgay was born in 1914 in Tibet (now part of China). He later moved to Nepal and lived with the Sherpa people. Sherpas, who moved from Tibet to Nepal hundreds of years ago, have lived in high mountains for hundreds of years.

Tenzing Norgay.
UPI—EB Inc.

Not far from Tenzing's adopted village rises the majestic Everest. It is part of the Himalaya Mountains and lies on the border between Nepal and Tibet. When Europeans went to Nepal to climb mountains, many Sherpas were hired to carry supplies for the mountain climbers. Because of their experience living in high mountains, they proved to be excellent guides and **mountaineers**.

At the age of 18, Tenzing moved to Darjeeling (Darjiling), in India. He hoped to earn his living carrying supplies for mountaineering expeditions. Three years later, he accompanied a survey team as a **porter** on an expedition to climb Mount Everest. During the next few years, he took part in more Everest expeditions than any other climber.

Working with so many different people, Tenzing learned to speak seven languages. Later he became a *sirdar*, or an organizer of porters. He continued to guide expeditions to Everest and inspired many mountaineers.

During their historic climb of Mount Everest in 1953, Edmund Hillary lost his footing and nearly died. Tenzing did not panic. He held the rope line tightly and planted his axe firmly in the ice. Later he simply said, 'Mountain climbers always help one another.'

For his courage and heroism and for having been one of the first people to scale Mount Everest, Tenzing was awarded the British George Cross and the Star of Nepal.

DID YOU KNOW?
Tenzing Norgay was the first man to be photographed on the summit of Everest. Since Tenzing could not operate a camera, Edmund Hillary took the photograph.

LEARN MORE! READ THESE ARTICLES...
FERDINAND MAGELLAN (VOLUME 4) • MOUNTAINS (VOLUME 1) • NEPAL (VOLUME 7)

Here, Edmund Hillary (on the left) and Tenzing Norgay prepare for one part of their climb to the top of Mount Everest.
Royal Geographical Society; photo, Alfred Gregory

SEARCH LIGHT

Fill in the gap: Someone who organizes porters for mountain climbing in the Himalayas is called a _____.

Answer: Someone who organizes porters for mountain climbing in the Himalayas is called a *sirdar.*

G L O S S A R Y

agent something that produces an effect

architect person who designs buildings and advises in their construction

aristocratic having to do with the upper social classes

aspect part, feature, or quality of something

astronomy the science of the heavenly bodies and of their sizes, motions, and composition

autobiography life story written by the person it is about

betray to lie to or go back on one's word

biologist person who studies living organisms and life processes

bond connection or friendship

boycott the refusal to deal with a person, group, or country, usually in order to show disapproval or to force a change in behaviour

Braille a system of writing for the blind in which letters are represented by raised dots

campaign planned activities designed to lead to a particular result

captive one who has been taken or held in a cage or as a prisoner

chairman person who leads a meeting or an organization

charitable done to serve the needs of the poor or sick

chemist scientist who studies the make-up and properties of physical substances and the changes that they go through

civil rights the social and personal rights of a citizen

commoner person who is not of the noble or upper classes

communism system of government in which all property is owned by the state or community and all citizens are supposed to have a share in the total wealth

conflict disagreement, struggle, or fighting

constitution document containing the basic beliefs and laws of a nation, state, or social group

controversial causing division or disagreement

crown prince (feminine: crown princess) the prince next in line for a crown or throne

culture the ways of life, traditions, and behaviours of a specific group of people

debut first formal public appearance

descendant member of a recent age group of a family or similar division that began years earlier

dictator person who rules with total power, often in a cruel or brutal way

diplomat person who works to keep up friendly relations between the governments of different countries

discrimination the treatment of some individuals or groups differently from others without any fair or proper reason

dynasty series of rulers of the same family

edict law or order given by a ruler or leader

element in science, one of the basic unique substances that make up all matter

emperor (feminine: empress) the ruler of an empire

evolution the process of changing, especially over time

exile official separation or removal

extremist person who holds unusually strong opinions or beliefs

foundation the support on which something rests; also, the base from which an idea or creation grows

geometric based on straight lines, curves, and simple shapes such as circles and squares

gory violent and bloody

governess woman who teaches and trains a child in a private home

guerrilla person who is part of an independent fighting force that makes surprise raids behind enemy lines

gymnastics difficult physical exercises, often performed as a sport in competitions

immortal living or lasting forever

imperial having to do with an empire or emperor

inspiration something that causes a particular thought, feeling, or idea

lens (plural: lenses) curved piece of glass that concentrates rays of light

liberation freedom

marginal lying at or near the outer edge (margin) of some larger place, object, or group

mesa flat-topped hill or small upland with steep sides

metropolitan having to do with a city and its heavily populated surrounding areas

migration movement from one country or place to another

monarchy form of government in which the ruler inherits the position and rules for life; monarchs include kings, queens, emperors, and tsars

mountaineer mountain climber

nature inborn or instinctive way of behaving or thinking

negotiate to discuss and bargain with another in order to reach an agreement

noble of upper-class birth or rank

non-fiction literature that is based on fact rather than imagination

nuclear weapon explosive device that produces enormous power by splitting apart the centres of the tiny particles called 'atoms'

pagan (adjective) non-religious; *especially*, used disapprovingly to describe a form of worship very different from a familiar and socially acceptable religion

parliament the lawmaking division of some governments

particle tiny bit or piece

persecute to treat cruelly or harmfully for an extended period of time; *especially*, to make a person or group suffer because of their beliefs

photoelectric effect electrical effect produced when light strikes a metal surface

physics the science that deals with matter and energy and the way they interact

plot the main story of a work of literature

pollen very fine dusty substance that comes from flowers; it is important in reproduction of other plants

pope the leader of the Roman Catholic church

porter person who carries baggage

prime minister the chief officer of the government in some countries

prism piece of many-sided clear crystal

pyramid structure with a square base and four sloping triangle sides that meet in a point at the top

rebel person who fights against an existing power or way of doing things

reign the time during which a ruler is in power

republic form of government in which the leader is not a monarch and is usually a president

rhythm regular pattern of sound

ruthless without pity

sabotage damage or destruction of property that interferes with an enemy's use of it

sacrifice valuable offering made to a god; *especially*, a human or animal victim killed on an altar

skyline outline of buildings or other large objects against the background of the sky

solar having to do with the Sun

sophisticated complicated or stylish

Soviet Union country of eastern Europe and northern Asia that existed from 1922 to 1991 and consisted of Russia and 14 other republics

species group of living things that have in common certain characteristics and share a name

strike temporary stopping of normal activities in protest against an act or condition

summit top or highest point

tapestry heavy cloth that has designs or pictures woven into it and is often used as a wall hanging

technique special way of doing something; *especially*, the way a skilled individual handles the details of an art or craft

theory in science, an idea or reasoned explanation for why things are as they are or why things happen as they do

troupe company or group; *especially*, a working group of stage performers

vow solemn promise or statement

wages payment for work or services